THE BEAUTY OF A DARKER SOUL

The Beauty

of a

Darker Soul

Overcoming Trauma Through
the Power of Human Connection

Joshua Mantz

LIONCREST
PUBLISHING

THE BEAUTY OF A DARKER SOUL
Overcoming Trauma Through the Power of Human Connection

ISBN   978-1-61961-674-5 *Paperback*
       978-1-61961-675-2 *Ebook*

PUBLISHER'S CATALOGING-IN-PUBLICATION DATA
Names: Mantz, Joshua.
Title: The beauty of a darker soul : overcoming trauma through the
power of human connection / by Joshua Mantz.
Description: Austin, Texas : Lioncrest Publishing, 2018.
ISBN: 9781619616745 (pbk.) | 9781619616752 (ebook)
Subjects: Iraq War, 2003-2011-Personal narratives, American. |
Veterans-psychology. | Post-traumatic stress disorder-Patients-
United States-Biography.
Classification: LCC RC 552.P67 M37 2018 | DDC 956.70443

Contents

"Hope is like a road in the country; there was never a road, but when many people walk on it, the road comes into existence."

—LIN YUTANG

Foreword

By   Ken   Falke

JOSH MANTZ HAS TOLD HIS STORY ABOUT DYING ON
the battlefield to more than a million people. In this book,
Josh shares his second near-death experience for the first
time.

Label it what you want. Some may call it PTSD, moral
injury, survivor's guilt, depression, anxiety, but I call it
LIFE. Trauma doesn't single out one person. Every one of
us will experience ups and downs, from birth until death.
Battlefield trauma affects our minds and bodies the same
way that any trauma does.

Josh tried strategies that many others have used in
dealing with the trauma, pain, desolation, and despair. He
helped others, engaged in a small dose of therapy, abused
alcohol, and sought comfort in relationships. Ultimately,
Josh came to realize that there is only one answer for what

ails us-making the treacherous and often perilous journey into the dark corners of our own soul.

It is in those dark corners that we find out what is true for us, what drives us, and what hurts us. As Joseph Campbell said, "It is in the abyss that we recover the treasures of life."

Josh's story of rebirth, a second time, is a reminder of the power of times of deep struggle, and of a decades-old science that is the focus of nearly every moment of my life: Posttraumatic Growth, or PTG.

PTG is the name for the journey from deep struggle into profound strength, growth, and service. When you achieve PTG, you find those treasures in the abyss-as Josh did-and experience stronger and deeper relationships, new possibilities, an increased sense of appreciation for life, increased connection to your spiritual or religious life, and a greater sense of personal strength.

As you walk your path of life, two things will ensure that you can avoid just riding the ups and downs of life and thrive, rather than just survive. First are wellness practices, like meditation, exercise, reading, and breathing, which will ensure that you keep your head and heart connected and can regulate your thoughts, feelings, and actions. Second, and perhaps more importantly, is deep, meaningful, and genuine human connection. This isn't about your electronic friends, but the small, inner circle of people who inspire, motivate, and challenge you to be the best version of yourself each and every day. In this book, Josh talks about some of the mentors and guides in his life, from therapists to Vietnam veterans, who are the only reason he is still with us to tell his tale.

We live in a world beset by loneliness, hopelessness, addiction, and suicide. A world filled with pain and hurt people who hurt people. Josh's story is a reminder of the power of personal connection, empathy, listening, and old-fashioned hard work.

As you read this book, rather than lionizing Josh for his incredible experiences and harrowing journey, compare his struggles to those in your life.

Never forget that the human condition is universal and that the things that we share in common-a desire to be seen, heard, and validated-are far more powerful than our differences.

—KEN FALKE, PHILANTHROPIST, FOUNDER AND
CHAIRMAN OF BOULDER CREST RETREAT

Introduction

The Darker Soul

IF YOU'RE READING THIS INTRODUCTION BECAUSE you've experienced trauma, then you know.

You know that during the normal course of any day, there are people who find themselves pulled violently from their normal world. They're plunged into the dark side of human nature and the worst circumstances that fate can hand them.

You also know that it often happens in a heartbeat, but when they return to normal life everything is different. Their perception of the world seems irreversibly stained.

They push through life, day by day, trying to act as normal as before. But nothing seems to work and they don't understand why. They feel dominated by a deep void within themselves that seems impossible to relate to. Impossible to overcome. Impossible to describe. They feel dead inside.

It impacts every aspect of their lives, and they just want it to go away.

Months, years—even decades—go by as they resort to almost anything to overcome the void. Yet, for some reason, it seems to keep deepening, becoming more dominant and controlling. Many start believing that something must be wrong with them, while the void they are trying so hard to resist starts to define them. They feel they have a darker soul, a growing distance between themselves and the feelings of normalcy they once knew.

What you might not know is that the most challenging aspect of recovery often begins with the recognition of trauma's moral, ethical, and spiritual wounds. These emotional wounds—which include things like shame, guilt, betrayal, and powerlessness—are the deep roots of chronic traumatic distress. The promising news is that these wounds *can* be overcome. Over time, they can actually add significant depth to the meaning and purpose of our lives. I know because I've been there. I have a darker soul.

You might have already heard my story. One hot April afternoon in 2007, I was leading my platoon on a patrol in the streets of Baghdad when I was shot and killed by a sniper.

While receiving emergency medical care, I felt myself succumbing to death. I could feel my body reacting, trying to save itself in spite of overwhelming blood loss. I struggled to maintain consciousness, repeating the names of my sisters and my mom over and over. My final thoughts were completely focused on them and my hope that they would be okay.

I felt no pain, no fear. In fact, I felt safe. It was a pure, peaceful calm. I knew what was happening. When the moment came, I took my last breath, thought one more loving thought of my family, and I died.

I had flatlined. Minutes went by. The medical team worked diligently. At six minutes, when most would have accepted the inevitable, they continued to give me CPR and life-saving drugs while trying to jolt my heart back to life with a defibrillator.

At ten minutes, eleven minutes, twelve minutes, it was obviously all over. But the team continued to work on me. Finally—a full fifteen minutes after I began to flatline—they detected a faint pulse.

Against all odds, they had brought me back from death. And against even greater odds, I managed to come through it with my brain capability fully intact.

I shouldn't be here. I died in Iraq. Simple as that. But as remarkable as it was to experience this and return to life, it paled in comparison to the decade-long emotional struggle I endured as I sought to find meaning in a "second life."

Many assumed that my brush with death would have given me a newfound appreciation of life; but, in reality, I felt nothing. I was emotionally dead. My life was dominated by the same void I described above, and I desperately tried to reach for anything that would help me fill it. Because I couldn't place my finger on what was causing that void, I found myself traveling down many false and dangerous paths for nearly a decade afterward. It took over my life and I was no longer in control.

But most people never would have known that about me. And what's even more dangerous is that *I didn't even know that about myself* at the time. In the larger public's eye, I was a testament to resilience. I excelled in my career and dedicated my life to helping other people. But behind the scenes and in isolation, I was collapsing.

It took me nearly ten years and a lot of false starts to even begin to understand the depth of the void and the level of control it had over my life. But once I began to see the truth behind trauma, the genuine healing process began. The crippling feeling of isolation dissipated and I found meaning within the suffering.

Perhaps most importantly, I didn't do this alone. Even in my darkest moments when I felt most isolated—moments where I truly believed nobody could understand the depths of my pain—there was *always* someone in my life who proved me wrong. They were often people who had darker souls of their own. Overcoming their experiences enhanced their ability to help others do the same, just as it would ultimately help me in this very way.

For those who've experienced trauma and continue to feel plagued by that dark void, my hope is that this book will help you recognize and validate the source of your pain. As simple as this may seem, the complexities of our experiences can be very misleading and difficult to understand. I've found that this crucial first step in the healing process is often overlooked.

This isn't a war story. I took great care to use my military experiences as a vehicle to demonstrate a larger conceptual understanding of trauma, one that I hope is relatable to anyone. We all have a unique path in life, and it takes everyone to make this world tick. While we may have a natural tendency to compare ourselves to others, I assure you that trauma does not. As you read this, I challenge you to look for the deeper meaning embedded throughout the text as it pertains to *your* life.

It's important to be emotionally engaged to understand the depth of these concepts. The first section of this book is intended to do just that. I'll walk you through the details of a harrowing near-death experience and the profound insights that came with it. This section will also begin to shed light on the most vital aspect of this book—that trauma isn't always what it seems. Next, I'll take you through the ten-year journey that led to my emotional collapse, highlighting the near-fatal pitfalls that I encountered along the way. Then, in Chapter 12, I'll provide you with a synthesis of the most crucial concepts that kept me alive along the way. While the internal battle I fought through to reach this point in my life was extremely difficult, I came to see that the struggle was absolutely worth it. I hope to help you do the same.

This is a journey of finding beauty within the darkness.

Chapter 1

The Student

I WAS BORN AND RAISED IN SUNBURY, A SMALL TOWN in central Pennsylvania on the Susquehanna River.

One of my earliest memories was the passing of my father when I was very young, just barely in grade school. Obviously, that was a devastating loss at such an early age. But when I look at the big picture, I ultimately have to count myself fortunate. A couple of years later, my mother married a police officer named Degg Stark, who became the most influential role model in my life. He stepped in and took on the responsibility of a family: my mother, myself, and my younger sister who was about five at the time.

I never called him "Dad," he was always "Degg," but I couldn't have more respect for him.

Degg had been an infantry officer in the Army. After his service, he joined the police force and eventually became one of the top detectives in Pennsylvania. Toward the end of his twenty-five-year career, he reopened a murder investigation that had been a cold case for three decades. The files contained thousands of pages of interviews, but he just wouldn't let it go. That bulldog diligence in his character had a big impact on my view of how to conduct myself in life.

At one point, I had the idea to get into police work, but Degg steered me away from that. He'd seen so many young officers join the force believing they were going to do big things and rid the streets of crime. But reality isn't quite so straightforward. Those good intentions get stifled by cold reality and a bureaucratic legal system that ties everything up in knots. Degg knew how frustrating it was to collar a hardened criminal with a record and then see him go right back out on the street because of a minor technicality.

Police work can also be an incredibly harsh life. Day after day, police officers deal with terrible situations: cases of spousal abuse, child molestation, violence, and all kinds of trauma. They're constantly surrounded by negativity, with no positive counterbalance. You see similar kinds of horrible things in the military, but in police work it's a daily, year-in year-out grind. The moral weight of the challenges that officers face are extreme over time.

But Degg never brought those dark issues home with him, and I respect him so much for that. He was a serious guy and you could tell he carried around some heavy baggage, but he never did it in a way that was projected on us. He was just a good family man. He and my mom developed a tight relationship and, even today, they continue to grow closer, which I find more remarkable with each passing year. Almost every weekend they made it a point to take us out hiking or to do something like that together as a family.

Degg was also a pilot. He wasn't a commercial airline pilot, but he had just about every rating in the book for single and multi-engine aircraft. He taught flying in his spare time and started taking me up when I was still pretty young. I had my pilot's license by the time I was seventeen. I'd be the kid in school who took girls on dates in a little Cessna 150, instead of going to the movies.

But the one way that Degg was most influential to me was his approach to his work. Degg is a big guy, 6'4" and about 250 pounds, mostly muscle, so he's an intimidating presence without even trying to be. When I was a kid, I just assumed he was kind of a badass at work. Later I came to see that he was much more complex than that. He would get tough and intimidating when it was called for—he could turn that switch on in a heartbeat if he had to. But most often, he used empathy to resolve tense situations. With his calm demeanor, he would make a human connection to get to the root cause of an issue.

That made a big impression on me. I eventually came to see that Degg's empathy was also a core value of counterinsurgency; a concept that would soon become so important in my military experience and my life in general.

Once, when I was at Fort Riley, Kansas, I was on a jury

for a murder trial. The prosecution thought they had a slam dunk case, but there were huge holes all through it. I just applied the meticulous review of the details that I'd seen Degg use so many times. I ended up influencing the rest of the jury to come back with a not-guilty verdict. Later, I found out that the defendant had a prior conviction in a case that was almost identical. Of course, I instantly doubted what I'd done. But when I talked to Degg about it, he said, "Josh, it's better that ten guilty men walk free than one innocent man go to jail." He said he'd used that as a guiding principle his entire career. That's a perfect example of the many ways I've been influenced by his compassion and rock-solid judgment throughout my life.

So I grew up with a really good perspective of police work. I was also surrounded by family members in the military. It was Degg who first suggested that I might consider going to the United States Military Academy at West Point. I was about twelve at the time and I was a pretty serious kid. I wanted to be an athlete and a good student. And I liked the idea of going into the military. Degg pointed out that I could do all three at the Academy. Once I locked onto that concept, I was focused on getting into the Academy from the first day I set foot in high school.

To get into the Academy, you have to start applying your sophomore year. You have to be completely dedicated and focused on it or you won't make it in. None of this was imposed on me by my parents. They never pushed.

They were great role models, and because they trusted me, everything I did was self-driven. I was never out partying or doing drugs or anything like that.

My level of focus naturally led to leadership roles. Throughout high school I was the captain of the football team. I also wrestled, did some track and field, and played on the baseball team. And I was heavily involved in our Junior ROTC Program. By the time I was a senior I was leading that program, which included about two hundred students.

I was popular in high school, but Junior ROTC wasn't exactly a magnet for the popular kids. You had to wear a uniform to school once a week, so the perception of the military was there. Also, a lot of kids who were less fortunate would join the program. For some reason, I found myself naturally dedicated to helping kids who had a harder go of it. I wanted to help them gain a sense of purpose. I was always like that, and that natural commitment really drove a lot of my leadership within the program.

That's where I met the second huge influence in my life: Sergeant Major Doug Van Der Pool. Doug had been in the 7th Special Forces Group, which was responsible for South America. He was there at the height of the drug wars and he had incredible stories about fighting drug lords and building rapport with citizens and the local military forces. His mission was predominantly based in counterinsurgency doctrine and my introduction to that type of military intervention came from him.

DEVELOPING RELATIONSHIPS AND TRUST

When you think of Special Forces, you might imagine direct action operations, the kind of stuff you see in movies. Doug was an expert at that too, but his main focus was counterinsurgency and he was somewhat of a legend in that regard.

Counterinsurgency is considered by some to be the graduate level of warfare because of its complexity. And, it's a paradox. On one hand, it has to be aggressive in weeding out lethal insurgent operations. But on the other, it's a military operation that's dedicated to protecting average citizens from the hardships of combat in their neighborhoods.

That's why counterinsurgency success hinges on developing relationships with the local population. You have to earn their support and trust. You might have 5 percent of that population that's extremist, bent on terrorizing and undermining the existing government. And then on the opposite end of that spectrum, you have a 5 percent counterinsurgent force that's trying to stop the extremists. The 90 percent of people in the middle are just like normal people anywhere else in the world. They want to raise families and live in environments where their kids can walk outside without getting injured by a mortar round or a roadside bomb. They just want to live peaceful, fulfilling lives without ever having anything to do with combat or war. Those who travel a lot probably understand this. People are just people, regardless of where you go in the world.

Doug taught me the crucial importance of humility in counterinsurgency. He stressed that you have to remain humble with the people who live where you're deployed. You have to respect them for who they are and understand that they have an incredible capacity to survive and succeed in spite of their hardships. He especially impressed on me the importance of understanding the language and the culture. But that's just the start. You also have to build relationships with community leaders, school teachers, and people who run businesses. You have to be a city mayor and an economist. You have to learn how to negotiate and understand governments and social structures.

All of these things and many more are essential for building relationships. Then, in addition, you have to be a tactical expert to make counterinsurgency successful. It's not quite the image that most people have when they think of the military. But Doug instilled in me the importance of counterinsurgency, and that quickly became my focus when I thought about a military career.

So, here's this legendary counterinsurgency expert. He retired, came to a small town in Pennsylvania, took over a high school Junior ROTC program, and he just ran with it. But he was still really well connected, so he'd do things like land Chinook helicopters in the front yard of our high school and take the young Junior ROTC cadets off to field training exercises at National Guard bases. We'd be doing night land navigation, obstacle courses, rappelling, and all the stuff that even college ROTCs couldn't normally do.

It all added up to an incredible experience for myself and a handful of other cadets Doug took under his wing. He spent a lot of time mentoring those of us who were clearly on track for a military career. He was always there for me and became a very close friend. He instilled in me a lot of the same rock-solid values I picked up from Degg. But Doug really drove home the importance of understanding other cultures and languages, and then respecting them with humility.

Under Doug's mentorship, high school became a rich experience that culminated with two important moments. The first was at home. My mom and Degg had a child together—a little girl named Kendra. This was a big deal for our family, a really happy moment for everyone. I was in my senior year, so, because of our wide age difference, Kendra's been a mix of a little sister and a daughter to me. Even though I was away during most of the years she was growing up, she's been a special part of my life.

The second big moment was the one I'd been focused on for several years: I was accepted at West Point. I can't overstate how happy I was. With West Point, you don't just send in an application. You go through multiple interviews and separate application processes. You also have to get a nomination from one of the Congressmen from your state, and I was fortunate enough to get two. It was a long, intensive process that paid off with the incredible feeling that the opportunity of a lifetime was opening up. And the experience is kind of a whirlwind. You report to the Academy just one month after high school graduation. When you hop on that train, you never get off. Before you know it, you're immersed.

But then, everything changed in a heartbeat.

A DEEP SHIFT IN CULTURE

Just a few weeks after I'd started at the Academy, in the middle of a class one morning, someone came in with stunning news. It was almost impossible to comprehend. A jet had crashed into the World Trade Center.

Like everyone, we felt this shock deeply. Then the second plane hit. Then the Pentagon. That one really jarred us. It felt personal, like a hit on our home base. Hours later, we learned that the fourth plane had crashed in Pennsylvania, just 150 miles from my hometown—that hit me heavily.

On the surface, very little was disrupted at West Point because of 9/11. The Academy is all about discipline, so the TV was quickly turned off that day and we pushed forward with the mission at hand, which was continuing with our class work. We knew that there was little we could do about it in that moment, but we were all thinking the same thing: this is the first shot in the war we're going to fight. It caused a deep shift in the culture of the Academy as we went about our routines. A new level of seriousness and focus started to sink in.

My class at West Point—the class of 2005—is actually nicknamed "The Class of 9/11." That's because we were the first class after 9/11 to take the Oath of Reaffirmation. This is an oath you take after your freshman year. You're basically saying, "I've been here a year. I understand the serious gravity of our work. Now I make the commitment to see it through."

We were the first class to make that commitment knowing we were committing ourselves to joining the war on terrorism. It carried serious weight. The reaffirmation isn't just a commitment to finish four years at the Academy. It's also a commitment for five years of active duty service, then eight years of reserve service, minimum. By taking that oath, you were essentially volunteering to lead men and women into war.

The Academy is academically challenging; but, after the invasion of Iraq in 2003, the struggle became even more challenging. For myself, and I know for many of my fellow classmates, there was a nagging sense of guilt. We felt like we should be out in the conflict. It was very difficult for me to remain in that academic environment and not go downrange with everyone else who was over there. Degg, and others, talked me through that, urging me to be patient and stick it out at the Academy. And I did. And I'm glad I did. I wasn't ready yet.

HONING SHARP INSTINCTS

West Point uses a unique academic method called the Thayer Method. Colonel Sylvanus Thayer is known as "The Father of West Point." The key idea behind his method is to teach officers *how* to think, not *what* to think. To do this, he reversed the typical academic technique. At the Academy, you're expected to read the assigned material prior to class, then you're tested on it as soon as you walk through the door. Only after that does the teacher go over the material in detail.

It seemed like an odd way to do it, but after I graduated I understood the value in that approach. It teaches you how to pick up a manual and learn from it on your own. In fact, it was kind of a throwback to what I'd been doing a few years earlier when I studied old communist era books from the 1960s about counterinsurgency. That was all I could find on the subject at the time. The Thayer Method trains you to innovate and take on the responsibility for learning and figuring things out for yourself. That was perfect training for the counterinsurgency environment; later, in Iraq, we had to learn on the fly. It was mostly on-the-job training.

What surprised me most about West Point was the minimal emphasis on military training. Most of your grade, more than half, is based on academics, with roughly 35 percent based on physical fitness, and the other 15 percent based on military proficiency. With this stunning reality, I decided to participate in a couple of different groups that were much more military oriented, like I was. We spent a lot of time involved in activities to help sharpen our tactical skills outside of what we were already required to do. I had a strong desire to become the best tactical person I could be.

From a military standpoint, I was very focused—driven to be one of the top cadets in class. But academically I struggled, especially at the beginning. I remember my very first class was called Discrete Dynamical Systems. To this day, I still have no idea what that means. But I managed to pass. And things got better. In the last couple of years I made the Dean's List, but the academic side continued to be challenging.

By my sophomore year, I'd decided to major in Arabic. After 9/11, it was clear that our military focus was going to be in the Middle East. That decision was largely influenced in high school when Doug emphasized humility and the importance of building one-on-one relationships with people. Familiarity with the language is a big part of that. So, instead of mapping out a career and choosing a major like engineering or working toward an MBA, I was exclusively focused on my five-year military commitment. I knew that being able to speak Arabic with the local population would be a huge advantage when it came time to lead a platoon somewhere in the Middle East.

One of my Arabic instructors at the Academy was Colonel Mark Conroe, a dedicated teacher and mentor. At one point, my work in his class was faltering. He took me aside for a long talk. Most of his Arabic students were going into the military intelligence community, but I was one of the few who was going to be on the ground as an infantryman.

What he told me stuck with me. He said, "You're going to be in Baghdad before long and a kid is going to be running down the street yelling, '*Qunbula! Qunbula!*' and you're going to know that *qunbula* means bomb. That might allow you to save the lives of your team and everybody else around you. That's why this language is so important." His words fired me up again and redirected my focus. He was so right, of course. I ended up using Arabic to our advantage every single day I was in Baghdad.

Mark was the instructor who taught us Al-Fatiha, or "The Opening." It's the first passage in the Quran. It's a long passage, but Mark insisted we all learn it verbatim. He said, "This will save your life in the Middle East."

He knew this because he'd served in the Middle East as a foreign area officer. That's a key strategic post in US embassies around the world. The FAO is a regional expert who provides a bridge between foreign governments, their militaries, and our American counterparts. If there's a crisis in the region, the Pentagon calls the FAO. In fact, Mark was the FAO in Yemen when the USS Cole was bombed. He was one of the first people they called to stabilize that crisis. So, the scope of his perspective as an Arabic teacher was invaluable.

And just like Doug had done back when I was in high

school, Mark emphasized the importance of humility when conducting business in foreign regions. Those two things—humility and knowing the language—turned out to be more powerful than any weapon I ever carried in Baghdad. They were indispensable.

During my whole time at West Point, I was torn about the fact that I was studying while other people I knew had enlisted to serve immediately. One of my best friends at the Academy withdrew during our freshman year. Like me, he had a strong military focus, so he made the call to drop out of West Point and enlist. It was a tough call to not go with him.

Another close friend, Brett Swank, had enlisted right after high school graduation. I went to the Academy and he went straight into the military. After 9/11, I really wanted to follow his lead and enlist, but my family and instructors strongly advised me to stay the course, reasoning that, if I waited, I would be more effective later as a well-trained officer. I saw the logic in that, but it was very hard to be patient and hang back.

One night during my senior year, I was in my room writing a history report when I got a call from an old friend. He had terrible news. Brett had been killed on a patrol in Baghdad. He was hit by shrapnel that severed an artery. That blow hit me hard. Here I was close to graduating, and all I wanted to do was drop everything and enlist. But once again, I got through it by relying on a network of friends, family, and senior officers at the Academy. I was just twenty-one and pretty headstrong, but they urged me to have patience and not throw away everything I'd worked so hard for. I had to develop a blind trust that finishing school was the right thing to do.

One of my instructors helped me arrange to attend Brett's funeral. I missed two days of classes, which is something they rarely allow. There's no class skipping at West Point. But they let me go home to Pennsylvania for the funeral. It was extremely emotional, of course. This was just three years after 9/11. There was still a strong feeling that we were united as a country, and that showed through. It was moving to see so many people in our community come out to show support for Brett's family. Police cars and fire trucks escorted his funeral procession. Hundreds of people lined the streets.

That level of support, that was the moment that inspired me to lock in and finish West Point so I could be as effective as possible when I got to Iraq. This was in 2004, and it was clear that the war wasn't going to end anytime soon.

A GREAT PLACE TO BE FROM

West Point is such an intense experience that it feels surreal to find yourself sitting in the graduation stands. You spend four years immersed in such a concentrated, regimented schedule that it's hard to grasp that it's coming to an end.

You don't realize the person you become at the Academy until years later, when you finally see what you're capable of. One of the jokes among graduates is that West Point is a great place to be *from*, but not a great place to *be*. It takes some time to fully understand what it teaches you and how it changes you.

Like any graduation, there was a sense of relief and a festive quality to it all—but I wasn't feeling that. It didn't seem like I was crossing a finish line. It didn't even feel like an accomplishment; I was focused on the next steps. There was nothing about graduating that outweighed the fact that Brett had been killed and other friends were downrange, engaged in combat, while I was still sitting there, trying to be patient.

My family was there, of course, along with Doug Van Der Pool, my Junior ROTC instructor from high school. Maybe the best thing about those last days was something that Doug told me. I think he must have sensed that my mind was far away, already down in Fort Benning, Georgia, where I would soon be starting one year of infantry training.

We were sitting at a bar, catching up over a Jack and Coke the night before graduation, and Doug said, "When you get to your platoon, the first thing to say is, 'I know *nothing*.'"

He meant that figuratively, but it was perfect. I was a second lieutenant with a strong base of leadership skills, but I was still unseasoned. In one year, I had to be ready to walk into a platoon of experienced, top-notch soldiers and become their leader, while still learning as much as possible from them. Young officers fall flat on their face if they don't bring some level of humility to that environment. You have to start humble, build relationships, and inspire trust.

I know nothing.

That was exactly what I needed to hear at exactly the right time.

Chapter 2

The Soldier

RAGE, KAOS, AND DISORDER.

Those were the call signs for three of the squad leaders in my platoon. Call signs are simple names used for radio communication, and the call signs for these three men were coined because of the extreme, high-intensity combat they'd seen in previous deployments.

During one of those deployments, Rage was on patrol when a grenade tumbled into his path and detonated right in front of him. Despite being severely wounded, Rage got right back up, chased down the insurgent who threw the grenade, and killed him. It was only after the situation was stable that he sought medical attention. His entire body was peppered with so much shrapnel that doctors couldn't remove it all. He tells me that, to this day, he'll be in the shower and sometimes hear metal tinkling on the tile as tiny bits of shrapnel continue to work their way out of his body. This is how he got the name "Rage"—a call sign literally born in blood.

It goes without saying that Rage is as tough as they come. But the guy is a true gentle giant. Rage and his fellow squad leaders, Chaos and Disorder, were all quiet, confident professionals. They were humble about their expertise and the challenging situations they'd taken on and mastered, picking up a number of well-earned medals along the way. Each of them could turn it on in a heartbeat and brilliantly execute any mission they were called to do.

These were the types of seasoned soldiers I eventually had the privilege to lead in Baghdad. But before I could take on that level of responsibility, I required a full year of serious seasoning of my own.

ONE CHANCE TO GET IT RIGHT

When you walk out of the Academy, you leave with two things: a commission as a second lieutenant in the United States Army, and a bachelor's degree in your field of study. Since I elected to join the infantry, the next step for me was heading to Fort Benning, Georgia, for one year of intense infantry-specific training.

Finally, here was the boots-on-the-ground military instruction I'd been expecting, but never really got at West Point. It was often grueling, but I was eager to learn how to be an effective soldier and leader, prepared for anything.

From Fort Benning, I went straight to Fort Hood, Texas,

where I met my platoon for the first time. It was the summer of 2006. That was a huge moment. I had flashbacks of Doug Van Der Pool's message to me as I walked in the door. I was nervous because you only have one chance to get a first impression right and gain the trust of your team. That was my responsibility alone, not anyone else's. It all comes down to your personality, your demeanor, your selfless leadership. I knew I had to go in and tread lightly to learn about them, and learn *from* them more than anything else.

First I met the company commander, Jeff Morris. He told me straight out, "You're about to take over the best platoon you can possibly imagine." He wanted to size me up and make sure I would be a good fit. This unit was near and dear to his heart; he had been deployed with them, so wanted to impress on me that they were the finest soldiers he'd ever known. As I would soon find out, he was absolutely right.

This was the reputation of Rage, Chaos, and Disorder, and the men they commanded in their individual squads within the platoon. It was fairly daunting, to say the least. They were all older than me and had all proven themselves in combat. As a first-time platoon leader, I was faced with a steep learning curve. The interesting thing is that if experienced noncommissioned officers are good, they typically consider it a responsibility and even a source of pride to develop their lieutenant. Many consider it part of their job to groom and build strong leaders.

That was the mutual bond we began forming as we headed out the next day for the National Training Center in the Mojave Desert—an intensive, one-month simulation of combat operations. This was the perfect time and place to jump in and start building a foundation of trust in a harsh environment.

It certainly helped that I'm not the type of guy who goes in and tries to order people around. Wearing your rank to force an upper hand on your team is the worst possible thing you can do. Rank shouldn't really be much of a factor. If you're a good leader, your team is going to naturally respect and follow you. That's the ideal you aim for.

I'd already developed a personal leadership approach that recognized each soldier as a person first. Each individual has different things that motivate and inspire them, different concerns, strengths, and vulnerabilities. You have to weigh those things to bring out the best in each one, and then harness it to drive the entire team toward a collective objective.

For me, that objective was to prepare us for a counterinsurgency operation.

EXPERTS OF THE FIRST DEGREE

As I've said, counterinsurgency is highly complex because you have to build relationships to earn the trust of people from another culture. You have to learn their language, understand their customs and economics, respect their religious beliefs, grasp how they govern themselves locally and nationally, and then you have to have the insight to see how all of that influences their families and neighborhoods. And that just gets you started. Every community is different, every neighborhood, every individual.

In a way, I had to use similar tactics to break into this tight knit platoon and establish my presence as their leader.

The platoon was part of a company of about 150 soldiers that had previously been deployed in an area of Baghdad called Haifa Street. It was almost exclusively high-intensity conflict with firefights, tactical room-clearing operations, rocket-propelled grenades, and snipers—all of the worst that Baghdad could throw at a soldier.

This level of combat is the type you might see in a movie like *Black Hawk Down*. That's what they'd been doing almost every single day. From a tactical standpoint, there was nobody I'd rather go into combat with than that platoon. They were experts of the first degree. To have that kind of unit deploy together and then still be essentially the same unit a year later was very rare. Normally, members of the unit disperse after a deployment. They go on to different assignments, so the company gets broken up and rebuilt. But in this case, I had a tight, organic platoon that functioned on the level of a top-ranked sports team.

As you can imagine, it took great care to find my way into that team. After all, I was a green, twenty-three-year-old who had never seen combat, and I had to seamlessly transition this combat unit into a specialized counterinsurgency force, win their respect and trust while doing so, and not disrupt their powerful camaraderie.

Add to that the fact that the concept of counterinsurgency was not widely understood in the military at the time. The need to understand it was absolutely there, but it was sometimes hard to grasp for those who had been around for many years, and who were accustomed to formal military tactics like force-on-force fighting in a Desert Storm type of warfare.

A lot of them were masters of conventional fighting. But counterinsurgency was a whole new world to them. So, to build their trust, I constantly filled them in on the "why" behind this unique tactical approach. I used historical examples, going back more than fifty years so they could put it into context. Helping them recognize the past successes of other counterinsurgency efforts and how they could be applied in Baghdad was critical. They had to understand and internalize what we were doing. That was incredibly important, but I also felt I owed it to them. They'd be putting their lives on the line every single time we set foot on that road. They needed to be confident about what we were doing and know their efforts were valid—and not wasted in the least.

Most of them didn't understand counterinsurgency on the level I did or have quite the same passion for it. But they were supportive. They saw the importance of the strategic work I was doing, and I highly valued their tactical expertise. With that core of mutual respect, we became comfortable with our roles and made a lot of progress in just a few weeks at the National Training Center. We still didn't know exactly where in Iraq we would be deployed or the exact nature of the conflict we'd be walking into. But we did know it would be grounded in counterinsurgency.

The Army, as a whole, was just starting to make a formal shift toward making counterinsurgency operations a higher priority. Everything that I'd learned at West Point seemed to lean in that direction. We'd also had a little bit of exposure at the National Training Center. We worked with some interpreters and ran through scenarios where we partnered with native Arabic speakers to practice gaining their support.

But as we would soon find out, this was nothing even remotely close to going live in Baghdad.

You can do extensive briefings and trainings, but the nature of combat changes so rapidly that you can't fully predict what you'll be facing. You have to get there and actually move out into the sector to start experiencing it firsthand; that's when you get a feel for what needs to happen. We had reasonable assumptions of what to expect, but we had to be flexible—prepared to adapt. I'm confident that we did everything we possibly could to make ourselves ready. But the true test is combat, and that was always in the back of our minds.

GETTING A HANDLE

In October 2006, after about a month at the National Training Center, we were deployed to Iraq.

Our first stop was Kuwait. This is standard practice. Incoming soldiers spend a couple of weeks in Kuwait as sort of an adjustment and preparation period. While you're there, you verify that critical administrative paperwork are complete, like making sure your life insurance and other documents is in order. You also get a refresher of basic skills and training. Most of all, this stopover gives you a moment to adjust to the new environment of the Middle East so you don't have to acclimate in a combat zone.

The training during these couple of weeks was so basic that it was almost annoying. We all knew our stuff frontward and backward by then. We were more than ready and anxious to get to Baghdad. But one small moment during this phase of training still stands out in my memory.

An instructor was giving us a rundown on the different components of our body armor vests. When he got to the canvas handle on the back of the vest near the neck, it was pretty clear that it was a carrying handle to make it easier to lug around this sixty-pound vest. But it wasn't designed to be that kind of handle.

He said, "This is actually a dragging handle. If one of your soldiers gets injured or shot, you can grab this handle and drag them to safety."

That little detail was sobering. I didn't really give it a lot of thought, but noted it and hoped I'd never need to use it.

GREEN YOUNG MAN IN THE GREEN ZONE

When our deployment day arrived, a series of helicopter flights landed us at Baghdad International Airport. I remember the moment I stepped out of the helicopter, putting my boot on the ground in Iraq for the first time. I looked around and took a deep breath of the dry desert air. I actually felt a sense of relief. For years I'd known that I was headed here. I studied and prepared for it and spent countless hours thinking about it, imagining how it would feel. Finally, we were here.

Today, looking back on that moment, it almost strikes me as funny. The airport was in the Green Zone, which was highly secured at that point. In comparison to the place we'd be going, the Green Zone didn't really pose much of a threat. I think of it now and have to laugh at how inexperienced I was. But I wouldn't be green for very long.

We were transported to FOB (Forward Operating Base) Rustamiyah in eastern Baghdad. This was very close to Sadr City, which was arguably the most violent area in Baghdad at the time—during one of the most intense periods of the decade-long war.

I spent the first couple of weeks in Baghdad navigating a massive learning curve. Before I could even think about doing any type of counterinsurgency, I had to go out with my platoon to begin to understand the "basics" of the area. It was an explosion of information; I was eager to grasp it and connect all the pieces together. We had to learn the safest routes for driving, the threats to be aware of, the current targets, the friendly personnel, and so many other details.

Imagine going to a big city where you've never been. Think about how long it would take to fully figure out that city until you felt comfortable moving around without needing a map or asking for information.

Now imagine doing that with roadside bombs going off. A wrong turn could be fatal.

One of our first patrols out into the sector turned memorable when three car bombs exploded just a few blocks away from us. It was an attack on an Iraqi police station. Even from our distance, the explosions rocked us pretty good. Huge plumes of black smoke rose over the neighborhood. I wanted to rush to the scene immediately and check it out. It was intense. The adrenalin was pumping. I must have been a little too excited because one of the squad leaders quickly put me in check. He pulled me aside, grabbed me by the collar, and said, "Wipe that *fucking* smirk off your face...sir."

Every lieutenant needs a great non-commissioned officer like this. That brought me back to the ground. And it was needed. It was appropriate. This wasn't a game or a training exercise. My squad leader was experienced enough to know that there was much more to what was happening than just three car bombs. A different type of energy came over him that I hadn't seen before. You can bet that sunk in and I never needed to be thumped like that again.

One of the first nights we were there, a rocket landed close to our barracks—it shook us. Like the car bombs, this was a wakeup call, loud and clear. I wasn't frightened, but I looked to my right where our company commander, Jeff Morris, was sitting. I could see it barely phased him; he calmly stood up to check out the situation. Instinctually, I mirrored his reaction, which kept any fear response at bay. He was very accustomed to this and I followed his lead.

Jeff's calm but decisive demeanor and leadership style drove the culture of the entire unit. He had the trust of every person on the team and was the type of leader that we'd follow to hell and back without even thinking about it. He would come to face many incredibly complex situations and devastating losses throughout the deployment, but somehow continued to keep his composure and inspire the team to move forward every single time. Where my squad leaders developed me from the bottom up, leaders like Jeff developed me from the top down. It was this "synchrony of development" that allowed me to adapt to the new environment so quickly.

That said, most of us were new to counterinsurgency. At that point, if I had been thrown into a true conventional fight, I would've been caught flatfooted. Any force-to-force situation becomes a chess game of tactics and maneuvering. You have to know the ranges of your weapon systems and how to apply them for maximum effectiveness. Then you have to integrate those systems together with split-second decisions. I'd had some exposure to that and I could do it if needed; but, I didn't have anything close to the level of "real world" expertise that the Desert Storm era commanders had. You saw the result of that. A couple of days and that war was over.

The difference here was stark. There was no force-on-force. No conventional war. No front line. The enemy was hidden all around us.

GLIMPSE OF THE FUTURE

Early in our deployment we were partnered with the Iraqi National Police Brigade. They had their own small base in the middle of Baghdad. One of my first reactions after meeting with them was that we should be living out there with the police, not just driving in to visit them every couple of days.

I suggested this to my superiors, making the point that to really develop rapport and trust with the police and other people in the sector, my soldiers needed to be on a first-name basis with them. That one-on-one level of human connection is invaluable when breaking down cultural barriers. I knew the best way to do that would be to live *with* them on their military base.

That might sound radical, but it can be an effective counterinsurgency technique. There's a certain level of danger at first, but, when you're embedded within the population, you can build meaningful relationships faster. They come to see the human in you, and you see it in them. That's powerful. And you quickly find that it usually makes you safer, not less safe.

At this point, the Army was just making the transition from force-on-force fighting to full-blown counterinsurgency operations, so the idea of living with the locals still seemed counterintuitive to most. The idea wasn't picked up right away, but within a year or so it would be, and the success of it would become obvious.

TALKING THE TALK

Our first couple of weeks could be easily summed up in one word: violent. We took heavy mortar rounds and there were a lot of improvised explosive devices—IEDs. We were replacing a unit that had been hit very hard. Despite the way violence can rivet your attention, I had this deep internal belief that it was just one piece of the picture. I can't explain why. Maybe it was the nature of how I was raised and who I'd become, but I felt that success in this type of environment hinged less on tactics and more on building trust with the population.

I don't think the rest of the people in the platoon shared my level of confidence at that point, especially with us getting hit so hard. But I had the advantage of a different perspective; I was able to speak Arabic. Every time we were out on patrol, no matter what violent distractions were going on, I was able to at least attempt to speak with Iraqis in their native language. This helped us make an instant connection—you can't help but cut through cultural barriers and connect on a human level. I was able to go beyond the violence, almost feel the energy of the people. I firmly believe that's the most powerful tool we have in our lives, the power to make a human connection.

I have to admit, though, there were bumps along the way.

On one of our first patrols, I said something simple to an Iraqi man in Arabic, something like, "Hello, how are you? Did you see where this person went?" He just looked at me for a moment, and said, "Are you speaking English?" I laugh about it now, but at the time it was truly humbling. Here I am, a West Point graduate who majored in Arabic, and this guy can't even tell what language I'm speaking!

I knew I wasn't close to being fluent. Arabic is a complex language with several different echelons. The most formal is Quranic Arabic, which is used in the Quran, of course. The Quran is actually a poem that's traditionally sung. The only people who speak or sing it effectively study it and perfect it over their entire lives.

A step down from that is Modern Standard Arabic, or MSA. It's the common language of the Middle East. Most everything is written in MSA. But it's not comparable to our everyday English usage. A better comparison would be Old English, something like Shakespearean style. While educated people understand MSA, it would be a bit odd for them to use it in normal daily transactions. But if you study Arabic in the US, MSA is usually where you start.

Once you master MSA, it's easier to pick up the dialects. The dialects are spoken, not written, although social media is changing that. Written dialects are becoming common on Twitter and Facebook. Iraq has its own dialect; I knew I had to start picking that up when I realized that the average Iraqi didn't understand MSA. The interpreters could understand me, and when I worked with foreign military officers or the Iraqi police, they could understand. Here, I had to shift gears and get up to speed on the dialect so I could talk to shopkeepers, teenagers, and average people on the street.

We ran into an incident early on that showed me how important simple communication could be. We were securing a mosque. We knew there was a threat there, but only had limited information, so we were on high alert. It was tense. At the worst possible moment, one of our vehicles accidentally hit the side of a wall in front of a house. The wall was just brick and mud and part of it collapsed. A woman came running out of the house, screaming at us. With the possibility of a firefight breaking out, we were afraid for her safety. I approached her to calm her down, but it seemed as if she was used to just being dismissed when things like this happened. When I started to talk to her in Arabic as best I could, her whole demeanor changed. She quickly calmed down and understood we were sorry for damaging her wall. As a small gesture, I handed her all of the cash I had on me. It was only about twenty dollars and wasn't enough to repair the damage, but the gesture was sincere and well received. Just like that, an emotionally charged situation was diffused.

Progressively, I got much better at Arabic. Every night, I'd spend time with one of our interpreters. I'd never smoked before, but I started smoking to make a cultural connection. I'd buy them cigarettes, then we'd sit and have a smoke while I studied the dialect in the most effective way—through natural conversation.

An interpreter almost always came along on our patrols. When we interacted with local citizens, I'd make the effort to be the one who talked to them. I'd have the interpreter stand behind me so, if I got stumped, I could turn to him and let him take over. Eventually, I became better at understanding and speaking the dialect.

What really mattered most was that I was the one making the initial effort to speak to locals in their language. They noticed.

THE OPENING PASSAGE

A few months into our deployment, we were looking for

a local sheikh who was rumored to be "neutral" about the US presence. We wanted to make contact with him, hoping we could budge him from neutral to friendly. Sheikhs are Islamic teachers who are very influential in their communities. They're kind of like local commissioners, but with a more religious tone than a political one. We knew it would be important to meet him and get to know him. He had a high level of influence over the population, but he seemed to be avoiding us, disappearing as soon as we heard he was around.

Keep in mind that in any area where the insurgency was active, associating with US forces was potentially dangerous. Oftentimes, insurgent teams would enter areas after we departed to kidnap and torture those who worked with the Americans. We understood this fear, so we didn't press too hard. But we were always on the lookout for this elusive man.

Then one night, we literally bumped into him. We were on a late patrol when we came into a little square where he was talking to a couple of other Iraqis. He couldn't really flee because, when he turned around, we were standing right in front of him. He was clearly the man we'd been looking for; he was wearing the black clerical vestments of a Sheikh.

This wasn't really the best moment for us to finally find him. We almost always had an interpreter with us; but, that night we didn't. I started speaking to him in Arabic right away in the friendliest demeanor I could muster. I could tell how scared he was by the look in his eyes. So, almost without thinking—like it was a normal reflex—I began reciting the Al-Fatiha, the opening passage of the Quran. My Arabic teacher at the Academy, Mark Conroe, had told us that knowing the Al-Fatiha might save our lives one day. While it wasn't exactly a life saver that night, it clearly had a strong effect on the sheikh.

It was as if every barrier suddenly dropped. It was actually kind of funny. He spoke limited English, so right away we were doing our best to communicate in a crazy mix of English and Arabic. We both stood in the square, scratching our heads and trying to make sense of this disjointed conversation. But it worked. All in all, it was a very productive meeting. Just one week later, we were back smoking cigars with him in his house next to a mosque. It turned out to be a surprisingly strategic friendship; my unit was never attacked in that area again. Reciting Al-Fatiha didn't save our lives that night, but it may have helped protect us throughout the rest of the deployment.

It's hard to find a better example than that of the power of building relationships, just by demonstrating cultural respect.

THE STREETS WILL RUN RED

Obati was a Baghdad neighborhood on the outskirts of our sector. One day, we received a disturbing report from their local council saying, in effect, "If the Americans walk into Obati, the streets will run red with blood." When that report came in, we looked at each other—Rage, Chaos, Disorder, and myself—and we all said the same thing: "We need to go to Obati."

We had to see what this was all about—if it was a real threat or a bluff. We knew there was potential for a rough firefight. Going in, we were extremely focused, knowing the danger could be deadly serious.

On any normal patrol, my soldiers were expert tacticians who surrounded me while I talked to Iraqis on the street, in shops, or in their homes. They would give me a time limit. When time was up, they would come get me. They would literally force me if they felt we were too exposed. Staying in one spot for too long posed a major risk.

For the Obati patrol, we knew the control had to be textbook to minimize the chance of tactical error. At most, I would have only a couple of minutes to talk to someone on a corner, then we'd have to move on. Our mindset was disciplined and focused.

We arrived around midday, and, right from the start, it was intense. We got very hostile looks from people on the street. Americans had not been in their neighborhood for years, so we were met with a mix of curiosity and intimidating stares.

When we stopped our vehicles, I got out and approached a man and began speaking to him in Arabic. The hostility melted away immediately. To our surprise, the grim faces lit up with big smiles. We deliberately walked right through the middle of Obati and found nothing but the nicest and calmest Iraqi people that we'd ever encountered. It was a completely uneventful walk—not a shot fired—and we developed some good relationships coming out of there. Needless to say, the streets did not run red with blood.

The patrol also gave me a perspective on the difficult day-to-day challenges that the Iraqi people were facing. In most places, there was no electricity or proper sewers. Trash filled the streets, with rivers of raw sewage running down each side. Obati was hit particularly hard. When we first walked in, we saw young kids and teenagers knee deep in raw sewage, attempting to dig new trenches by hand. The people were doing their best to repair their community with the limited resources they had. It was a dire situation, and our approach that day was to find out how we might be able to help.

I'm sure when most people think of the war in Iraq, this is not at all what they imagine. On that day, and many others, we found that the combination of language and respectfulness was more powerful than any weapons we carried with us. When we got back to base and had lunch, we were relieved, of course. Even though we avoided a firefight, the stress of that patrol had nearly the same impact on our physiology. Sometimes, it's not the fight that has the biggest physical and emotional impact; it's the *threat* of one. We had to laugh at how uneventful this potentially dangerous patrol turned out to be, as our bodies returned to baseline and crashed, but it was an eye-opening experience to understand how successful a counterinsurgency mission could be.

FINDING ORDER IN CHAOS

As my platoon became adept at building relationships with Iraqi organizations, it was a natural fit for us to partner directly with the National Police Brigade. But the National Police and the Iraqi Police were not well respected by the population. Corruption in both organizations was widespread and they were highly infiltrated by insurgents. It was chaotic. That's not surprising in the middle of a war zone, where administrative structures have been torn apart and the rules are haphazard.

Take a city like San Jose, California, for instance. You have a population of about one million, and roughly one thousand sworn police officers. This makes the ratio of police to civilian 1:1000. That ratio works well in a stable country with strong government systems in place to maintain stability. It's quite a different story in a war zone with shadow governments, violent insurgents, and religious factions at odds with one another. To secure an area like that, the ratio needs to be closer to 1:20.

This was another critical aspect of counterinsurgency operations. Building strong relationships with the people hinges on our ability to secure the population and give a reasonable assurance of their safety. I can't expect an Iraqi shopkeeper to disclose meaningful information about the insurgents if he's worried that his family will be tortured and killed the moment we leave town. This is a very real concern that cannot be overlooked. Again, most Iraqis are not "bad" people. Usually, they weren't deliberately withholding information from us because they didn't like us, but because they were scared for their safety. And I don't blame them.

To overcome this fear, we needed to partner with the local authorities. I was given the task of helping rebuild the police force in our sector, to encourage a strong relationship between the local and national police, and try to fashion an effective organization that could support that area. This is an important concept in counterinsurgency as well. Certainly, the Americans had to be much more on the forefront of things in the beginning, but Iraqi establishments had to step up to take the lead in these efforts and eventually control their own government. The Iraqi people needed to be the face of these operations.

Again, the way I started building that relationship was by sitting down in the Iraqi National Police commander's office and just talking to him in Arabic. This guy was incredibly timid and clearly worried about having us there. I don't believe he himself was corrupt, but he was rightfully frightened to take action against the insurgents because of their capability.

Just as I did with the men in my platoon when I first met them, I had to build trust with the commander and his men so we could gradually incorporate them into our patrols in the sector. I explained to him how important it was that they should eventually be the face of these missions. I incorporated them into our training exercises and had medics teach them basic medical tasks. Our soldiers drilled them in fundamental military tactics and room-clearing operations. Just the fact that our young soldiers were training with theirs created a bond, even when they couldn't fully communicate with each other. As that bond developed, some became friends.

I told them, "I don't care if you can't speak a word to each other, if you're hanging out and playing video games together in your downtime, that's a win." This alone is a valuable step in the right direction. It's all about relationships.

THE FORWARD ELEMENT

During the course of a year-long military deployment, all soldiers have to take a two-week leave. This rest period is mandatory and based on an assigned schedule. Shortly after the first of the year, I went home to the United States to visit my family.

When I returned to Iraq in February 2007, the battalion commander asked me to take over the cavalry scout platoon. This was a big honor. In a traditional infantry unit, or cavalry unit, the scout platoon is the forward element. They are tasked with being the eyes and ears for the entire battalion and work directly with the battalion commander and staff. It was extremely hard to leave my first platoon, but I was excited about the impact we'd be able to have with the scouts.

A scout platoon has a slightly different mentality than an infantry platoon. It's not to say that one is better than the other, but they each have different strengths. The infantrymen were the tactical experts, and necessarily more ridged in their approach. Had it not been for them, I probably would've been killed many times over. Their tactical expertise, discipline, and wisdom kept us out of trouble.

Scouts, however, are trained differently throughout their career. They are bred to be more flexible, more adaptable, and a little more willing to take risks. They often have to think and act outside the box in terms of their operations, and can collect intelligence and do whatever else is needed to accomplish their mission.

With the infantry platoon, I found it challenging to get them to adopt counterinsurgency principles. With the scouts, there was a full-blown counterinsurgency spirit, no holds barred. Many of them had a natural knack for it, and some had served in leadership roles in previous deployments where they drove these principles themselves. This took a lot of courage, as they were often "going against the grain" of conventional military wisdom. When I talked to them for the first time, I went over some of the 1960s era doctrines. Their first reaction was, "This is excellent! Let's go do it. How about we try it this way?" They were receptive and excited from the word "go."

Within days of taking over the scout platoon, I felt like we'd built a nearly instant rapport. Our mentalities were perfectly aligned and we were quickly up and running. We were willing to modify normal procedures when needed and just do what made sense in order to accomplish the mission. Anything we thought we should try, even if we weren't 100 percent convinced it would work, we were willing to take risk.

For instance, I made it a priority that every time we went out into the sector we would hand something out to the people. We'd hand out clothes, school supplies, and anything else we could give them to improve their lives even in the smallest ways. It was a tangible demonstration of respect and sincerity, and it went a long way in building rapport and lasting relationships.

I couldn't go out and promise Iraqis that we'd build a new school or rebuild a hospital or bring in new physicians. I would never promise anything that I couldn't deliver. But, if we could give them food and basic supplies, or make minor adjustments in the community, or keep them appraised on the progress of certain projects, that was critical. That's what builds trust. And that's exactly what we were committed to doing, every single day.

The people appreciated this enormously. They knew how difficult it was to do these things in a war zone where there were always terrible threats of roadside bombs. I had to put the lives of all my men on the line just to go out and meet with a city mayor or a school principal for a brief meeting. These small gestures became so important. We couldn't say with certainty that our efforts were paying off, but we had faith in the power of the relationships we were building.

BUILDING TRUST ONE SHIRT AT A TIME

When you're a soldier, your parents always ask what they can do to help. Most people send care packages and things like that, and this really helped us with morale. But when my own mom asked that question, I said, "Mom, if you really want to help, the best way is to help us build relationships with the Iraqi people. The way to do that is with clothes. I need school supplies and clothes. Can you ask friends and people in the community if they'd be willing to help out?"

She understood right away and, a couple of weeks later, clothes started arriving, followed by more clothes and school supplies. Literally, hundreds of boxes started arriving. Now, I should have suspected what she was up to, but she didn't tell me until years later about the wide scope of her efforts. She had started a nonprofit organization to collect clothes and other donations. She arranged for media ads and was interviewed on the local news. She just threw herself into it and the response was amazing.

My little sister, Kendra, got involved too. When I was home on my two-week leave, I went to her school and spoke to her kindergarten class about Iraqi kids who struggled because of the war. I was speaking to young children, so naturally the message I delivered was shaped around culture. Many Iraqi children slept on bare floors, didn't have much to eat, and certainly didn't have toys to play with. This was a subtle message to their class to help give them some perspective on why we were there—"to help the Iraqi kids."

Shortly after that, Kendra's entire school decorated shirts with handprints and wrote messages to the Iraqi kids. When those boxes started arriving, I looked through them and found the shirt Kendra had decorated. I wanted to deliver that one personally to one of the Iraqi kids. I actually took a picture of the little girl who got Kendra's shirt. It was ridiculously risky. We were in a high threat area at the time, but it was worth it. Kendra loved the picture and she proudly shared it with her class. She framed the picture and it's still displayed in my parent's house to this day.

This was a huge personal connection that transcended generations. Here, in the midst of this complicated, dangerous war, my hometown was reaching out to build a unique relationship with the community in our sector. It was a wonderful feeling to be at the center of that bond.

I can't help but wonder if things like this will somehow contribute to preventing conflict twenty years from now.

THE WHITE HORSE

In the midst of all this, I was always looking for clues that our counterinsurgency efforts were working. I felt certain that they were, but sometimes it's hard to see clear results. You have to take it on faith. But there was one moment.

One night, we were in a remote area of the sector where we'd never been before. It was pretty far away from where we would normally be. It was after midnight and I was just talking with this Iraqi guy on the street, practicing my Arabic. After a couple of minutes, he stopped and got this funny look on his face. Then, in perfect English, he said, "Oh, you're that American officer who speaks Arabic. I heard about you."

I was floored! Here I was, miles away from where we usually patrolled, and this random person on the street had heard about me.

When I shared this story with one of our interpreters, he laughed and told me that the Iraqis had a nickname for me. They called me Hisan Al-Abyad, which means "The White Horse." He explained that in the Middle East the horse is a sign of hope, a very positive image.

It was humbling to hear this—and a little intimidating too. But most importantly, it was a powerful confirmation that we were getting through. Our efforts were paying off.

Chapter 3

The Family

OF ALL THE IRAQIS I MET AND DEVELOPED RELATION-
ships with during my deployment, one family in particular
stands out.

At the very end of December, in 2006, we were on a
typically long patrol. It was noon and the weather was
sunny and pleasant, by desert standards. We were traveling
through this rundown neighborhood in eastern Baghdad,
an impoverished area where displaced Shiites were living
in makeshift huts.

Whenever we were on patrol, children would approach
our convoy to ask for food or water. Sometimes adults
would be with them. We rarely stopped unless that was
part of our specific objective. It was usually too risky. You
could never be sure whether someone might be trying to
draw you out of your vehicle and into an ambush to give
a sniper a clean shot.

This time, a middle-aged man came running up to

us. There was an open field to our right, and I could see him waving us down from about fifty yards away. When we got closer, I saw a look in his eyes that was so sincere and desperate that I made the decision to stop our convoy.

All four of our vehicles ground to a stop on the dirt road. Against the advice of my squad leaders, I climbed out of the vehicle so I could talk to him. I still hadn't quite gotten the hang of the local dialect, so our conversation was a jumble of broken Arabic. No matter. He made it clear that he wanted me to follow him to show me something.

This was much riskier than just stopping to talk, but my instincts told me to trust his sincerity. I sensed that whatever it was he was so adamant to show me would be important. In my short time in Baghdad, I'd found that a lot of Iraqis were abrasive and disgruntled, and rightfully so. But there was something in this gentleman's kind demeanor that compelled me to go with him. There's a look that people have when they've lost everything, when they're hopeless, and when they're completely vulnerable. It's not a look that can be faked.

A WARTIME TRAGEDY

I directed the platoon to come along with us and we followed him to his nearby home. I immediately noticed that more than half of his house was gone, reduced to rubble. Through our interpreter, he explained that American shelling had done this. He pointed to a piece of shrapnel embedded in the wall. I worked the twisted metal out of the crude plaster. Right away I noticed a US serial number on it. The evidence couldn't have been stronger. My stomach sank.

This presented a dilemma. On one hand, this was war. Situations like this can happen, as horrible as they are. They're regrettable and heartbreaking, but you have to live with this kind of bitter hardship. On the other hand, our success hinged on building trust with the population. This family was innocent, and dismissing their concern would do us no good. Our mission now was to rebuild these relationships to *prevent* things like this from happening again. I felt it vitally necessary to stay and extend him a helping hand.

I looked at him and, much to his surprise, told him he was right, this was a US round. I asked a few questions through our interpreter and he explained that the attack had hit his house just the day before. The first shell hit their sleeping room. Another destroyed their cooking shed. By then, the terrified family had clustered together in a corner of their compound where the third and final shell had landed nearby.

Two women were killed. Two more teen girls were so badly hurt that each of them lost legs to amputations. A four-year-old boy and his fifteen-year-old sister were also hurt. Their father hadn't been there—he was an Iraqi Army sergeant, stationed in Ramadi.

It was devastating to hear these details. This gentleman

was a cousin to all of the family members and was caring for them now as best he could.

I asked him if there had been an insurgent mortar team firing rounds from someplace near their home before the American attack. He said there had been, about ten minutes before the three shells fell. As he was saying this, he pointed to the insurgent team's location about twenty yards away. Now it was clear what had happened. Nearly every day, traveling insurgent teams would set up their mortars and fire on the US base. I'd been on the receiving end of those mortars. They land so frequently that you actually get used to them. Or rather, you desensitize yourself to the fear of them.

When insurgent mortars land on the base, our soldiers try to get a bead on the location of the mortar team. We don't counter-fire if the shells come from a populated area. In this case, fire was returned because our maps showed the area to be an abandoned garbage dump. In a tragic oversight, this little community of ramshackle huts was targeted because it wasn't even known to exist.

When I explained all this to the gentleman, he was surprisingly understanding, given the terrible loss to his family and their home. If he felt any anger, he wasn't directing it toward us or blaming us. I found that to be exceptionally empathetic on his part.

One of his family members, a young boy just a couple of years old, had a large wound on his leg that was starting to get infected. I directed our medic to go right to work on him, cleaning and dressing the wound. A teenage girl named Hajil had been caring for the little boy in the absence of their mother. She had a big smile on her face and seemed unusually composed, considering what had happened to her family.

When the medic started attending to the boy, the gentleman asked him to take a look at Hajil too. When she lifted the hem of her dress, I was shocked to see a large, deep gash on her leg that was clearly infected. I was really struck by that. Here she was with a smile on her face, caring for an infant, while at the same time she must have been in terrible pain. I couldn't help but be inspired by her strength and poise.

Before we left, I told them quite honestly that I couldn't promise I'd be able to do any more for them, but I would do everything I possibly could.

BREAKING NEW GROUND

Back at base, I shared this story with my commander and other officers. While I explained the situation, I also made the case for treating the family as part of a larger counterinsurgency effort in that area. Aside from the fact that helping this family was the right thing to do, it was also strategically important to rebuild trust with this population.

To my surprise and great relief, someone in the Army upper echelons made the decision to provide a condolence payment to this family in the amount of $10,000 USD. This was unprecedented in that area. They were breaking new ground.

We went out on a special patrol to give them the money. We had a chaplain along with us and a reporter from *Stars and Stripes*. Our medic spent some time, again, checking everyone out who had been wounded and I gave the family some of the clothes my mother had sent.

Through our interpreter, the chaplain spoke with the father of the house who had returned from his post with the Iraqi Army. The chaplain acknowledged that no amount of money could ever make up for their loss, then counted out the payment and offered it to the father on behalf of the people of the United States of America, in hopes that it could help the family in their time of need.

I was happy that *Stars and Stripes* was there so that this action could get wider attention. This was the kind of response that needed to be seen as standard procedure. It was an invaluable message to the community that we were willing to make amends when it was appropriate and reach out with humility and kindness.

When the chaplain handed over the payment, the father started to tear up, overwhelmed with emotion. We all sympathized with his tremendous loss. Personally, I am still amazed that this devastated family never once showed anger or tried to blame us for their hardship. In fact, they couldn't have been more thankful, understanding, and forgiving. In the midst of this tragedy, his forgiveness shook me. I learned from him that day.

In the *Stars and Stripes* article, I was quoted as saying, "I feel responsible for them all now." That really is exactly how I felt. They could've hated us, but they didn't. They displayed empathy and compassion, despite sustaining a severe trauma. In this case, it was the father who, through his compassion and forgiveness, formed an unbreakable connection with me. I was committed to them, and his response reinforced my belief that there are genuinely good people throughout the world, even in the most dangerous places on earth.

I wanted to go back to check on them, but I had to refrain. I didn't want to draw insurgents' attention to their family. As much as I would have liked to see how they were doing, I had to choose caution for their protection. This was an incredibly powerless feeling. I'll always remember them and frequently think about their well-being as their country continues to experience turmoil.

Chapter 4

The Interpreter

LIKE THE CHURCH BELLS WE HEAR ON SUNDAY MORNINGS in America, the Islamic call to prayer summons the faithful to worship. The call is actually a song with a beautiful, haunting melody. After a while in Baghdad, you get used to hearing it echoing through the streets five times every day.

One day, I was walking in Baghdad with Peter, the Iraqi interpreter who was most often assigned to our platoon. He was with us on an exploratory patrol to check out a mosque that was linked to insurgent support. The midday call to prayer was underway when Peter suddenly stopped and looked at me with a grim expression.

He shook his head and said, "We can't go any further." His face had turned white with fear.

I had a fairly good understanding of Arabic, but Peter's native ear picked up on a subtle change in the call to prayer that I never would have noticed. The call had turned into a recruiting message for insurgent militia.

Once Peter drew my attention to it, I was able to hear it. As we neared the mosque, they suddenly switched the message back to the call to prayer, probably because they saw us coming. Of course, this confirmed our suspicions that the mosque was an insurgent recruiting bed. Everybody in that area was suddenly suspect, and we now found ourselves caught in the middle of a very dangerous zone. This was not the time and place to get into a firefight. We were surrounded by high rises and thousands of people. A deep feeling of fear started to set in.

I could feel my body changing. As I glanced at my men, it was obvious that they were feeling the same.

Moments like this are frequent during combat; but, the thing that many people never recognize is the sheer power these events have over your psyche and physiology. Emotions like this are natural mechanisms to protect you from danger and increase the chances of survival. They are also the most difficult to overcome when you return home. The trauma isn't just about the act of getting shot or killed. It's about the *threat* of getting shot. Repeatedly forcing yourself to suppress that fear in order to function, while necessary in that environment, is one of the many factors that lead to severe emotional withdrawal afterward.

Our options were limited, so we decided to just go a little bit further and act as if we hadn't noticed anything. I continued shaking hands with people on the street, greeting them in Arabic, knowing that at any moment one of them might violently engage this American Army officer and his team who had dared to venture into insurgent territory.

We left the area as quickly as we could, keeping a casual manner and without incident. It's quite possible that Peter's sharp attentiveness was a life saver—for ourselves and many innocent people who were out on the street that day.

This is a perfect example of how essential a good interpreter can be. Their basic work is translation, but it goes far beyond that. If you want something translated, just go to Google and you're basically done. But good interpreters hear emotion. They read body language and facial expressions. They apply cultural understanding to every exchange. In addition to being smart and alert, they have to be intuitive. They pull all of this together to relay the most accurate message possible.

THE HIGHEST LEVEL OF LANGUAGE

Arabic is incredibly complex. It's known as a "fourth tier" language, which means, to a native English speaker, it's one of the hardest languages to learn.

The radical differences in the way the languages are structured makes translation exceedingly difficult. In Arabic, you often have to be able to interpret the totality of the sentence to understand the meaning of individual words. That takes a lot of practice, especially if you're drilling down into different dialects. Then, the reading and writing of Arabic is a completely different challenge, and a daunting one. It's read right to left, and the cursive style of the letters bears no resemblance to what we think of as letters.

This is what a translator is up against under the best of circumstances. That's why doing live interpretation is one of the highest levels of knowing the language; you have to be in a constant state of flow. It's similar to what athletes do. They lock in with intense focus, while also disengaging on some level to allow their intuition to inform them.

The amazing thing is that our interpreters did all this while constantly in harm's way. As they went about their normal duties on platoon patrol, any workday could explode with violence, and often did. When platoons came under fire or were attacked with roadside bombs, interpreters suffered the horrible consequences too. The one big difference was that interpreters work for years at a time with no breaks, while most US military deployments run about one year with mandatory breaks.

Why would they make such an extreme sacrifice? The easy answer is economics. Steady jobs were scarce in wartime Iraq. The urgency of providing for your family is powerful. But we also came to understand an even stronger motivation. They were driven by a desire to help their country heal and overcome the violent insurgency. This was their way of working toward the end of a wartime era so they could move forward with the hope of creating something close to the normal lives they once lived.

Years later, I met an Iraqi interpreter at Fort Riley,

Kansas. He showed me a video he had made in Baghdad before the war. I barely recognized it. It looked alive and vibrant, like New York City. There was no rubble, no bombed out buildings, no tanks in the streets. When I saw that video, I finally understood what our interpreters had been working for and why their dedication was unwavering. They simply wanted to get back home.

BALANCING TRUST AND FEAR

I can't stress how vitally important the interpreter's job is to a counterinsurgency operation. The ability to communicate is crucial in establishing a human-to-human connection and in getting past cultural differences. Without that human connection, there's no way to earn the trust which forms the bedrock of counterinsurgency operations. That's why we had interpreters with us on nearly every single patrol.

But there was another side to the interpreter program—a darker issue. Many Americans were reluctant to trust them. The fear was reasonable; it would be difficult to detect a corrupt interpreter. Though difficult in a war zone, the military conducted background checks as much as possible so that we could be fairly certain that an interpreter had no ties to the insurgency.

Still, there was the fear that an interpreter might purposely give false information, which would be impossible to confirm. You had to take them at their word, trusting that their interpretations of conversations with fellow Iraqis would help your efforts rather than undermine them. With our lives in the balance, there was a lot at stake.

There were several highly publicized events over the last several years in which foreign military personnel—our allies—turned against their American counterparts. They'd build up trust, wait until the Americans were vulnerable, and then kill them in cold blood. Although incidents like this were quite rare, the deep-seeded tension caused by this level of betrayal is impossible to forget.

Like so many others, I fought the urge to wrap all of our foreign counterparts into that same category. I held firm in my belief that most people are genuinely good; I refused to compromise our integrity because of the actions of a few vicious extremists. People like this don't define Iraq. They only define the actions of a very small population of fundamentally evil insurgents—and we had to find the strength to hold true to that.

Although it could never completely take away the possibility of a threat like this, having first-hand knowledge of the language helped. I could monitor conversations between our interpreters and the Iraqis, especially as I got better at understanding the local dialect. I knew generally what was being said. I found that this improved my interaction with interpreters. They came to trust me. I treated them as equals and built strong relationships with them. I think that encouraged them to contribute and feel as though they were an important part of the team—and they certainly were. Sometimes, this required me to take risks and place blind trust in their actions, but I never lost sight of the fact that *they* were placing blind trust in us as well. The courage to trust in the good of another may very well be humanity's greatest defense against evil.

This mutual trust also made them want to go the extra mile for me. In one instance, an interpreter saw a sheet of paper posted on a wall. He insisted we stop the convoy. He jumped out of the vehicle, raced over to the wall, snatched the flyer, got back in the truck, and we were moving again in less than a minute. The flyer turned out to be a brand new notice with major propaganda from the Mahdi militia. When we took it back and had it translated, it revealed recruitment information, dates, times, places—a trove of valuable information. I would never have picked up on that myself. Many situations like this proved that an interpreter was absolutely pivotal to our success.

This invaluable help on their part put them at great risk. When we went on patrol, they would wear face masks to conceal their identity. The fear—theirs, and ours too—was that if they were spotted and could be identified by insurgents, it would pose an enormous threat to their families and themselves. They took the precaution of living in a barracks on our base, rarely venturing out to visit their families. That's the extensive level of sacrifice they were

willing to make to support their families and win back
their way of life.

CHRISTIAN IN A MUSLIM LAND

After going out on our first few patrols with various
interpreters, there was one man in particular I really took a
liking to and we developed a close rapport. This was Peter,
the interpreter who spotted the change in the call to prayer.

Peter stood out among the other interpreters because
he was much older, probably around sixty. He actually
reminded me of Santa Claus. He was a little overweight,
his hair was completely white, and he always had a smile
to go along with his kind and humble personality. He also
happened to be Christian, which was not all that unusual.
You do find practicing Christians in Baghdad. It was one
more thing that set him apart from the other interpreters,
who were mostly young Muslim men and women in their
twenties.

To my mind, the division between Muslims and Christians in Iraq is somewhat exaggerated. I definitely saw
something very different there. Sheikhs hang out with
priests. Sunnis could be found with Shia'a. I even saw a
mosque coexist peacefully next to a church. Christians
were a small minority, of course, but their relationships
seemed amicable. I think this goes back to the idea that 90
percent of the population wants nothing more than to live
and let live. They want to go about their lives peacefully,

never raising a hand in anger, much less guns and roadside bombs. The religious extremism in the Middle East is clearly driven by a relatively small group of zealots dead set on imposing their indecent values on everyone else.

It was that 90 percent who had the potential to be our allies. They were the ones we worked so hard to win over so that Peter and his family, friends, neighbors, and their communities could live in peace.

"GO WITH GOD"

When I first worked with Peter on patrol, I asked him to stand behind me and listen whenever I tried to speak to someone. I would do everything I could to make the conversation work; but if I got stuck, I wanted Peter there, listening, so he could step in and help me. This quickly became frustrating. I had to turn to Peter quite a lot in the beginning.

After one of our early patrols together, I took Peter aside and asked him if we could spend some time just chatting in Arabic so I could get a better handle on the language and the local dialect in particular. I was dismayed that I wasn't able to communicate better, but was totally committed to doing everything I could to improve my Arabic.

So, one night after a patrol, I brought some cigarettes to his barracks. We sat and talked. Peter described different intricacies of the Iraqi dialect. I responded in the dialect as I slowly picked it up. We would often just talk about whatever popped into our minds. All these years later, I don't remember specifics of exactly what we talked about, but I remember that these late-night sessions came to feel like a refuge.

We were always exhausted after patrolling, which typically went on for ten or twelve hours. But once we got settled, lit a couple of cigarettes, and started to talk, everything changed. Here we were, in the middle of this intense war zone—a harsh, complicated environment—and we were able to detach from it all. When we began talking, all the tension and the trauma of the day stepped aside. It was like a safe haven, far removed from the war. Heavy responsibilities seemed to lift away. Whatever time it was seemed irrelevant. We could breathe easy. The talk flowed. We'd have a laugh, then the next minute the ideas would go deep. There was a sense of peace to it all, just talking about whatever came to mind between this old Iraqi man and this young guy from the other side of the world, brought together by the most unlikely circumstances—we found a connection through language and through these moments of sharing our human experiences.

During one of those sessions, Peter taught me a simple phrase that still means so much to me: *Fe ma' Allah*. Roughly translated, it means, "Go with God." It's Iraqi dialect and it's a kind way to say goodbye to someone—one with an implied blessing in it. Years later, when I was studying Modern Standard Arabic, I would throw that out to some of my instructors when class was over. They would always stop and ask me where I'd learned that, and I'd tell them the story about Peter.

Fe ma' Allah. Go with God. I don't believe I would have ever learned that if it wasn't for those late night sessions with Peter. To this day I still use that phrase when I interact with people from the Middle East.

LIGHTING THE PATH

I built relationships with most of the interpreters because of my ability to speak Arabic, and because I treated them like the vital partners that they were—but I was closest to Peter. In just a few weeks working together, we got to be good friends.

One morning we were preparing for a patrol when my company commander, Jeff Morris, took me aside. He had terrible news. Peter had been assassinated. Jeff knew that Peter and I were close, so he wanted to tell me as soon as the report came in.

Peter had left the base to go home and visit his family. He was just a couple of miles down the road when a car slowed down beside him and an insurgent in the car shot him twice in the head—a classic drive-by shooting. A local patrol happened to be nearby and they were able to take some photos to verify Peter's identity.

Jeff had the photos with him. He asked me if I wanted to see them and I did. It was clearly a head shot, so I was relieved that his death was quick. There were many cases where insurgents tortured people in public. They used terror to send a message to any Iraqi who might think about assisting Americans. I took some comfort that Peter had been spared that horror.

I was deeply saddened, of course, but I wasn't overly emotional. When you're at war, you expect death and violence daily. For better or worse, your mind has to be open to that. It's going to happen. There's no maybe. And it can just as easily be you as someone else. My general attitude remained in combat mode, naturally suppressing the emotion in order to function. I knew that getting emotional would do no good for me or Peter or my men. We moved on and continued preparing for the patrol.

But before he left, I did tell Jeff one thing. I said I wanted to give the eulogy at Peter's memorial service. We always had a memorial on the base for any soldier who died in combat. Peter was the first interpreter to be killed since I'd been there, so I was immediately committed to take the lead on his service and give the eulogy in Arabic, followed by an English translation.

This was a way to show the highest respect for Peter. I soon came to see that it could accomplish much more. It would show respect to the other interpreters, which was critical. They took all the risks that we did, in addition to another layer of risk for their loyalty to us.

I wanted to do it for the Americans too. There was such

a divide between many of the soldiers and the interpreters. I wanted this to be a way to help overcome that divide so we could work more closely together and reach a higher level of success. And finally, I was hoping that for me, an officer, to get up before our entire battalion and do this in Arabic would help nudge our unit forward in understanding the importance of language in this environment.

Fortunately, the battalion commander was fully supportive. I didn't mention to him that there was one small problem—I wasn't quite fluent enough in Arabic to pull it off. So, the night before the memorial, I went to the interpreters' barracks and said, "Guys, I need your help writing this eulogy. It's going to honor Peter, so it's got to be perfect."

They couldn't have been more helpful. Immediately they were all smiles and rallied around to get started. There were about seven interpreters helping out, some of whom I'd worked with during patrols, and others I didn't even know were jumping in to assist. They started throwing out ideas and sharing what they knew about Peter. That's when I learned Peter's real name, Armanak. Peter was his code name. Out of respect, and partly for safety, I'd never asked him for his real name. In fact, I incorporated into my speech that I had just that day learned that my friend Peter was better known as Armanak.

My crew of interpreters helped me create the speech of my life. It turned into a beautifully crafted Arabic eulogy that almost read like poetry. As I delivered it, it all hit me and I became emotional. When I'd heard about Peter's assassination, I was in combat mode, preparing for a patrol—I was all business. But at the memorial, in front of all his peers, his absence was suddenly glaring. I realized how much of a sacrifice he made, and it both angered and saddened me. It was difficult to get through, but I did.

I don't remember all the details of the speech. It was handwritten and that copy was misplaced during the chaos after I was shot. But I remember one line in particular, one part of a sentence that I thought was a beautiful description of Peter's sacrifice. It read, "Peter gave his life in order to light the path of freedom for the Iraqi people." That one line has stuck with me ever since. It was right on the mark. It really captured the devotion that Peter and so many others, American or Iraqi, brought to their work.

The turnout for the memorial was also a high point. There's usually not a mandate for anyone to attend a memorial service. Since it was for an interpreter and not a soldier, I was wondering what the attendance would be like, but that wasn't a problem. The battalion turned out in force and completely filled an auditorium that seated about five hundred. It was a packed house. That show of respect for Peter deeply inspired me.

After it was over, our battalion executive officer came up to me with tears in his eyes. He said, "That was fantastic. That was exactly what was needed." He was one of the key officers who I had been able to talk with about counterinsurgency, and was a true mentor. He really got it and was always supportive. He also understood how important our interpreters were in making a connection with the Iraqi people. All in all, it was one of the most gratifying moments of my Army career.

To this day, it still humbles me when I think of the selfless dedication of Peter and the other Iraqi men and women who served the US as interpreters. My respect for them couldn't be greater. Often, when I think of them, and when I think of Peter, I send up the little blessing he taught me, *Fe ma' Allah*.

Chapter 5

The Sniper

WHEN I WAS AT WEST POINT, I READ A BOOK CALLED *Ghost Soldiers* by Hampton Sides.[1] The author wrote about Lieutenant Henry G. Lee, who was held prisoner by the Japanese during World War II. Under the worst imaginable conditions, he survived the Battle of Bataan in the Philippines and then the Bataan Death March. While fighting at Bataan, he started writing a diary with poetry to distract himself from the relentless daily horrors he experienced. Sometime after his death, his notebook was discovered stashed under a prison hut. The poems jolted me, making a lasting impression. One in particular stood out. It's written as a tribute to Mars, the Roman God of War:

Drained of faith, I kneel and hail thee as my Lord,
I ask not life, thou need not swerve the bullet,
I ask but strength to ride the wave, and
one more thing, teach me to hate.

1   Hampton Sides, *Ghost Soldiers* (Anchor Books: New York, 2001), 37.

I'm not sure why, but I had that poem scrolling as the screen saver on my laptop the whole time I was in Baghdad. The energy of the poem seemed to match that of the environment we were in.

I don't remember when I first had the idea of incorporating part of the poem into a tattoo, but when I went home for my two-week leave in early 2007, it seemed like the perfect time. What can I say? I was still just a kid. I was feeling bold. I came up with this intricate design of a vulture with a spear and trident (all three are symbols of Ares, the Greek counterpart to Mars), with the word "Ares" written in Greek letters underneath. And then, on my arm, I had the tattoo artist lay down this phrase from the poem that resonated deeply with me: "thou need not swerve the bullet."

To me, this line meant "bring it on."

I distinctly remember an incident shortly before I went on leave that explains this feeling quite well. We were traveling down a main route in Baghdad during a mission when my lead vehicle made a call over the radio telling us to stop immediately. I looked to my right and saw a cinder block amidst a pile of trash directly beside me. It was slightly discolored and had all the signs of being a roadside bomb. The problem was, we were right beside it. It was one of the most intense moments of fear I experienced throughout the war. We were in the kill zone and there was no possible way out if it were to detonate. Somehow, I found a way to harness the fear by staring directly at it, almost daring it to blow up. Fortunately, it didn't. That was one of the key moments early in the deployment where I started to feel "larger than life" and stopped caring about living or dying. After a while, my fear surrounding incidents like this all but completely dissipated—and I felt like I was at my best.

Emotional suppression becomes a necessity to not only survive, but thrive in chaotic situations. It also brings dire consequences during the recovery process. It's extremely difficult to regain control of our core emotions after we've become so accustomed to suppressing them, and it's somewhat addictive. If we reach a point where we no longer fear death, it evokes a strong feeling of freedom that's difficult to break away from.

Just a few weeks later, I would learn the moral of this story: don't tempt the God of War.

TAKING THE LEAD

When I returned to Iraq after my leave, I was surprised and honored to have the new assignment to the battalion scout platoon waiting for me. It was exciting to be among so many who were receptive to counterinsurgency and to trying new techniques. I missed the camaraderie I shared with the men in my old platoon; Rage, Kaos, Disorder, and other soldiers are among the finest I've ever known. The scout platoon, however, allowed us to take a quantum leap in counterinsurgency initiatives. These efforts sparked quick changes.

My commander was willing to let us try almost any technique that made sense and was grounded in historical results from other counterinsurgency programs. For me, this new flexibility was like a blast of oxygen. I worked directly with the battalion staff and my team to plan strategies that we hoped would have the most effective impact. On our patrols, while we began handing out clothing and school supplies on a daily basis, we also launched other new projects throughout the sector. I had the freedom to take the platoon almost anywhere in the sector where we would do the most good.

Our biggest change was our relationship with the Iraqi Police.

In Iraq, you have the National Police, which is basically designed to be the equivalent of our National Guard. Then, separately, are the Iraqi Police; and while they *should* have been the equivalent of a local police force, they were nothing like our police forces in America. "Rag tag" would be a good description. "Ineffective" would be another. They wore police uniforms, but they were poorly trained and weren't well respected. At times, they didn't even have fuel for their vehicles. Just let that irony sink in! Here they were, in one of the most oil-rich countries in the world, and they couldn't get a tank of gas to do the critical work of a police force in a war zone.

Nevertheless, I knew it was important to gain their trust and make them our allies. Along the way, I knew we could help them sharpen their military skills.

Now that we'd been given a much stronger mandate to mount counterinsurgency measures, the idea of living with the Iraqis became more realistic. The time was right and we made arrangements for the scout platoon to set up a barracks at the police headquarters in the middle of our sector, which was a very rough, high-risk area of Baghdad. We lived there for a few days each week, then we'd return to our base for the rest of the week to reset.

On our days back at the base, we'd run our regular patrols. When we operated out of the Iraqi Police headquarters, we partnered with the police for joint patrols. I made sure we ran as many of those patrols as we could, and every time we went out I wanted the police to be recognized as the face of it.

We were operating right in the middle of the community, and that's exactly what we wanted. We had less driving distance, we could spend more time out in the sector, and I felt we were much safer, taking fewer risks on access roads that could be riddled with explosive devices. Most importantly, we were right there, side by side with the Iraqis, and that was the perfect place for building our relationships with the police and the community. Every day, we moved a little closer to the goal of having the police take the lead on these patrols.

Throughout this period I spoke Arabic almost exclusively. When my soldiers were asleep, I'd often go over to the police chief's office to just chat with him. One evening, early on, they invited me to their private area for a meal of chicken—similar to rotisserie chicken—with naan bread that was cooked over a wood fire on the street corner. The fresh naan in Baghdad was just incredibly delicious. I didn't have an interpreter with me, so our conversation that night was somewhat broken, but we loosened up and had some laughs. These were the simple things that started deepening the relationship.

UP ON THE ROOF

During this time, I felt braced with a great sense of liberation—but there was an awful lot of pressure too. My mind was constantly racing as I wondered what we could do to solve the massive, complex problem of undoing this relentless insurgency. How could we have the greatest impact as a unit? Who do we need to build a relationship with? What area would be the best to visit next? Am I doing enough? What am I missing that I should be doing? My brain was always going like that, a hundred miles per hour.

Our barracks were cramped quarters at the police head-quarters. During our down time, the soldiers would clean their weapons, write letters, watch DVDs on their laptops, or play cards or chess just to keep their minds busy and occupied and trying to stay sane.

Sometimes, with my mind spinning so furiously, I'd go up on the roof of the building where it was quiet and peaceful. Having that big sky above and Baghdad stretching out in all directions provided much needed solitude. It helped me calm down and put my thoughts in order. It was a perfect place to think, even though it actually wasn't safe up there. I was an easy target for snipers. Once it got dark, though, that wasn't as much of an issue.

I didn't go up there to sleep; but, at times, late at night, my mind would finally throw in the towel and I would doze off. Sometimes I'd wake to the sound of the call to prayer at 5:00 a.m. from the mosque next door. This beautiful, mysterious melody would arrive with the first light of dawn. It was a perfect way to wake up, with a sense of eerie peacefulness.

After a moment, I would take a deep breath and head back downstairs—back to my men, responsibilities, plans for the day, my mind starting in again, spinning, spinning, spinning.

THE ROCK

Marlon Harper was on his fifth deployment. He was a phenomenal soldier and a wonderful person. Exactly the person you'd want by your side in a tight fix.

Every person in that platoon looked up to Marlon because, from a professional military standpoint, he'd raised them all. He'd trained every one of them and they were all first-rate soldiers. Along the way, every one of them discovered the same thing about Marlon: he was fearless.

Marlon insisted on taking the lead on every patrol,

refusing to let anyone else drive up front where there was the highest risk of being hit by explosions from roadside bombs. These IEDs were our biggest threat while traveling. Occasionally, we'd get a sniper shot, but they were rare.

To make matters worse, the militia had recently developed a new type of roadside bomb called an EFP—explosively formed projectile. This merciless weapon was nothing more than a piece of copper encased in a cinderblock, with C4 explosive or propane attached. It was terrifyingly lethal. When detonated, the copper would flash to thousands of degrees instantaneously, turning into a mass of molten slug that could cut through anything in its path. It sliced effortlessly through armor, skin, and bone with devastating results. I was in an armored vehicle that was rocked by a nearby EFP—this was in a Bradley Fighting Vehicle, no less—and we were tossed twenty feet off the road as if we were in an empty barrel.

EFPs were easy to make and inexpensive, so we were hit with them frequently, sometimes more than once a day. For about twenty bucks, a small team of insurgents could wipe out a $20 million armored vehicle in a heartbeat. EFPs were also difficult to detect because insurgents would hide them in rubble, and there was rubble everywhere.

Yet, Marlon seemed to have no fear of roadside bombs. He stopped the patrol once because he spotted a cinderblock that looked suspicious. He got out of the truck, walked up to the block, tipped it with his foot, checked for wires, walked back to the truck, and said, "We're good." He was as calm as a guy walking in the park. If that had been an IED, and if it had exploded, he would've been gone. Literally, there would have been nothing left. He simply had no fear of them.

One night while were talking, I asked him straight out, "What's up with you and IEDs, Marlon? It's like you have no fear. You know what they can do. Why aren't you more cautious with them?"

He looked me straight in the eye and paused for a moment, like he was deciding whether or not to tell me; then he smiled ,and said, "I already got my calling, sir. And it's not an IED." He turned back to his laptop and kept working. That was it.

That took me aback. It was kind of spooky. Spooky enough that I didn't feel comfortable coming right out and asking what his calling was.

I later found out from my platoon sergeant, Eric Smith, that Marlon was petrified of snipers. He had absolutely no fear of IEDs, even though that was by far our biggest threat—but snipers terrified him. We rarely got a sniper threat, but when we did, he would almost turn into a different person. It's like he would collapse into a shell. He didn't become ineffective, but it was obvious he was preoccupied with worry.

I can't say that Marlon actually had a vision of how he was going to die, but his comment about his calling implied that he felt some kind of predestination. It would not be an IED. I had to wonder, was he thinking sniper?

TESTING THE LIMITS

Preparing for a new patrol, I showed the Iraqi police chief a map of an area where I wanted him and his men to accompany us. His face went pale and he became anxious. He shook his head and said, "That's outside of our sector. We can't go there. It's too dangerous."

Not only was it outside his sector, it was also across the street from Sadr City.

I knew about Sadr City, so I understood why the chief might be nervous about going anywhere near. This Shi'a district in northeast Baghdad was an exceptionally dangerous insurgent stronghold—off limits to most US personnel at the time. I had no intention of going in, of course, but there was a little square right on the border of the city where I wanted to get a foothold. It was high threat, but I felt that, as scouts, we had the opportunity to at least check it out, meet the local leadership, and find out what the needs were.

Before my meeting with the police chief, we had been up there by ourselves, just the Americans. We got a lot of hostile looks. Even when I spoke Arabic to the locals it didn't do much to break the ice. When we found the local leader, I spent some time talking with him, but he was skeptical. US forces had made promises to him before, then (in his experience) just disappeared, never to be seen again.

During this conversation, my interpreter discreetly informed me that some of the men in the leader's entourage were militia members. He was also picking up hostility from their sidebar conversations. We were not in a friendly spot. Still, I thought we might be able to change the tone, back it up by keeping a promise, and then start building a relationship.

In spite of the poor reception, I walked out of the meeting feeling cautiously optimistic about what we might accomplish in the long run. The locals clearly needed food, clothes, and supplies, so right away I started planning a second patrol to deliver what we could. I wanted the Iraqis to be the face of this operation to help foster trust between the local citizens and the police. This is where I was met with some resistance from the police chief.

With my interpreter helping out in this delicate negotiation, I explained to the chief how beneficial it would be for him to reach out to these citizens and begin building a relationship. We would supply the clothes and provisions that he would hand out, and we'd be on the patrol, of course, as an escort to protect him and his men. When he suddenly agreed to go, I was a little shocked. Originally, I hadn't been aware that the mission was outside of his sector. I was afraid that would be a deal breaker, so for him to agree to this significant commitment was a huge win.

CITIZENS, POLICEMEN, AND SOLDIERS

April in Baghdad is known as "bloody April." As the weather warms up, insurgents get more aggressive—more snipers, more bombings, more blood. But even when you constantly go on patrols and are frequently under attack, you don't really imagine that your own blood will be added to bloody April.

The early morning air was dry and cool on April 21, 2007—a typical start to another warm day in Baghdad. As the call to prayer echoed in the streets, we began prepping for our patrol.

But right away there was a glitch.

Marlon approached me with the bad news that we didn't have the supplies for the police to hand out. He'd forgotten to bring them in from our main base. He knew that the whole purpose of this patrol was the humanitarian drop, so he was frustrated and upset with himself, which wasn't like him at all. He just never screwed up like this. He was most troubled that the trip back to the base would put his men in danger on a road that was a high threat for IEDs. The success of the patrol we'd planned so carefully was at stake, so the round trip drive had to be made.

This posed an enormous moral dilemma for me, one that I still toil over to this day. It was a seemingly small situation, representative of the difficult decisions you have to make as a leader in a counterinsurgency environment.

On one hand, this was a critical patrol and the humanitarian supplies were the essence of it. We needed the Iraqi people to start trusting the Iraqi police. Although this was a baby-step in that direction, having the police hand out free supplies to the people in this area was a crucial first step in building that trust. Moreover, getting the police chief to agree to a patrol outside of his sector was a one-shot deal. This mission represented far more than a humanitarian drop. This was the mission that would solidify a tangible partnership between us and the Iraqi police. We couldn't just cancel it.

On the other hand, I was about to order my men to travel several miles down one of the most dangerous roads in Baghdad, and for what? To get some t-shirts and school supplies? Even the average soldier wouldn't hesitate to place his life on the line to save a comrade, but it can be difficult for them to understand why they have to put their lives on the line for a t-shirt.

This is the complexity of counterinsurgency. The paradox is that this patrol was, in many respects, as urgent and important as rescuing a fallen comrade from a firefight. In the long run, efforts like this would protect them, generate more stability, and allow the Iraqi forces to assume control of the operation. I had to think strategically, often trying to visualize an environment that was months and years ahead of schedule. And every day I had to balance the risk of "what could be" with the lives of my men.

Fortunately, the supply pick-up went without a hitch.

Harper and his team returned in less than an hour—but I can't help but think how I'd feel now if one of them were killed on that trip. Would that particular mission have been worth their lives? How would I have explained it to their widows, kids, and parents? I know many other leaders who struggled with decisions like this, some of which didn't turn out in their favor. These situations are just some of the things that plant seeds of shame, guilt, and betrayal into the human psyche.

Nonetheless, Harper and his team made it back, and we loaded up and headed out, along with two police vehicles, to the little square on the border of Sadr City.

In spite of the late start, the patrol ended up going remarkably well. I had the police hand out supplies from their truck beds as my men stood to the side. The neighborhood people were very thankful, almost swarming the trucks. At one point, I was up in one of the truck beds, Marlon was in the other, and we were fully exposed as we helped distribute supplies. I knew it was risky, but it was important to demonstrate this partnership between the citizens, the police, and the Americans.

There were a lot of smiles and expressions of gratitude. The city leader who had been so skeptical before seemed genuinely surprised and pleased that we returned as promised and fulfilled our commitment. I told him we would be back through the area sometime soon and we would talk again.

As we were finishing the drop, someone playfully handed Marlon a baby. This was too good to pass up. I took a photo of him with this infant in his arms. He had a big smile on his face. The morning glitch with the supplies was all but forgotten now, and our patrol had been a success. But as fate would have it, that was the last photo ever taken of Staff Sergeant Marlon Harper.

INTO HARM'S WAY

Right after I took the picture, I got a call from battalion headquarters. They needed us to immediately divert to another part of the sector. One of our units had been engaged by an RPG—a rocket propelled grenade—and they needed us to conduct a follow up search for insurgents in the area.

This presented another dilemma. I'd committed our platoon as an escort for the Iraqi police unit that was now in a dangerous area outside of their sector. They were taking a considerable risk at my request and I couldn't leave them high and dry. It would be a huge violation of trust and would compromise an already fragile partnership. It was my responsibility to get them back safely.

Our scout platoon was highly adaptable and I felt we could handle both situations. I made a quick decision to send two of our Bradley Fighting Vehicles to the intersection where the RPG activity was reported, while Marlon and I took two trucks to escort the Iraqi Police back to their headquarters. We'd then link back up after we dropped off the police, which would only take a few minutes.

This went off without a hitch. It seemed like everything was going our way that day. As Harper and I were getting ready to exit the police compound, we noticed a young boy selling deserts on a tray outside the police station. I gave him five bucks and Marlon and I ate as much as we could as we were driving out of the compound.

Just as we were leaving the gate, I got a call from one of our guys. He calmly said, "Hey, we were just engaged by an RPG. No damage. He missed us. But we were engaged."

Marlon and I flew. We tore through back roads and side streets to rejoin our platoon under fire. When we arrived, one of my men immediately pointed out the suspicious activity of a nearby car. When the RPG was fired, this car was moving very slowly just a block or so away. We suspected it might be an insurgent trying to videotape the attack. This is something they commonly did so they could show videos of successful attacks against Americans as propaganda.

My men had blocked the car off just as Marlon and I arrived. I got out of the truck and studied the area. It was a busy intersection right next to an electrical power station that was adjacent to Sadr City. It dawned on me we had actually been engaged by RPGs at this very intersection one time before. It was a prime spot for an attack because insurgents could fire at us from behind a wall at the power station, then make a quick escape through the backstreets of Sadr City. They knew we wouldn't give chase because of our orders to never enter the city. All in all, it was a dangerously open intersection.

When I went to check out the suspicious car, the driver turned out to be an elderly man, which didn't fit the typical insurgent profile. Sure enough, I spotted a high-quality video camera laying in the back seat. We got him out of the car and I began questioning him in Arabic as I looked over the camera, trying to get a playback on the viewer. At the same time, Marlon was doing a test on the man's hands to see if he had been handling any explosives.

At that moment, I noticed that Marlon was in a dangerous spot, wide open to Sadr City. I said, "Marlon, you're open. You might want to bump over to the other side of the vehicle."

"Yes sir," he said, "You're right. Good call." He took a couple of steps and walked straight into the crosshairs of a sniper's scope.

I only heard the muted shot of the sniper rifle. In that instant my sensory perceptions shifted. Dirt kicked up from my right and I thought we'd been hit by a booby trap or IED. I never would have thought sniper. Everything shifted to slow motion. I felt the vague impact of something hitting me. It felt like a tug—not much to it at all—but it seemed like my body was slowly absorbing it. It was almost like being lifted up by the swell of an ocean wave. Like a camera lens, my vision zoomed in on Marlon's eyes and with crystal-like clarity I saw a look of acceptance, as if he had known all along it was coming—this was his calling. His expression was calm. There was no fear, no wince of pain.

My perceptions were initially bizarre. Slow motion, fast motion, auditory distortion. As Marlon's body slowly fell to the ground, everything suddenly shifted to fast-motion. I grabbed the heavy canvas handle on the back of Marlon's body armor to drag him out of the line of fire, just like the sergeant told me to in Kuwait many months prior. He must have weighed around 250 pounds with all of his gear, but he seemed incredibly light.

As I was dragging him, I heard a voice that sounded submerged in water. It called for a medic. A moment later I recognized the voice. It was mine. I was on the radio, I said, "We have two casualties. Medic!"

Even though I spoke those words, it had not yet fully registered with me who the second casualty was. I knew Marlon was hurt severely, and everything felt so off that I assumed something had happened to me too.

I felt no pain or panic or fear. I just reacted. It was pure instinct. I began pulling off Marlon's gear. Buckles, straps, zippers—no thinking, just boom, boom, boom, it all came off. I called for our medic again, but my breathing was shallow and I could barely get the words out. I pulled up Marlon's shirt and stopped cold when I saw the hole in the center of his chest. Dark red blood was gushing out like a faucet. The bullet severed his aorta.

The proper thing to do would've been to immediately place pressure on the wound. But I didn't. It was my one moment of hesitation during this entire experience. In a moment that lasted no more than a second or two, I just stopped, with a frozen stare, and thought, "He's fucked."

My medic arrived while I was staring at Marlon's chest, but since I was kneeling down, he couldn't see my wound. He grabbed me by the shoulder and said, "Sir, who's the second casualty?"

I looked up and said, "I am."

My strength suddenly faltered. I fell over but didn't pass out completely. I was still conscious. Still alive. For the moment.

Chapter 6

The Medic

IT WAS AN ENORMOUS BULLET. YOU COULD HARDLY even call it a bullet.

We believe it was fired from a Russian anti-aircraft weapon that was converted into a sniper rifle. So this "bullet" was more like a powerful, vicious projectile. It hit Marlon's left arm, entered his chest, severed his aorta, exited the front of his chest, fused to part of his body armor, then ricocheted into my thigh, where it severed my femoral artery. At that point, it was a mutilated piece of metal the size of a fist. It literally blew up my leg, cutting through the artery and nearly severing the bone.

But I felt no physical pain. My perceptions were initially a jumble of disorientation. I could hear voices, but they were more like echoes of voices. My medic was there, I knew that. His name was Daniel. He was just nineteen years old. Imagine being a teenager and in the blink of an eye, you're put to one of the most difficult tests of your life.

He was young, but he was level headed, totally engaged, and he did everything right.

I was conscious throughout all of this, but it was like being awake on a subconscious level. I could hear everything happening. I felt no panic. I actually felt relaxed. It reminded me of being sick when I was a child and having that sense that everything was alright because my mom was there to take care of me. I gave myself over to her loving care, knowing I was safe. I felt my men pull me. I didn't even try to move. I was falling into a deeper and deeper sleep, slowing slipping away. Totally relaxed. "They've got this," I thought, "There's nothing else I can do."

But I could hear echoes of my men's voices struggling as they pulled me toward the Bradley Fighting Vehicle. There were a few small grunts and groans as they were dragging me. Then, one of my guys yelled out in a loud voice, "Come on, sir! Stay awake!" The urgent concern in his voice made me understand how traumatic this was for them, and it activated the last ounce of adrenaline I had left—and I needed it. I felt guilty for slipping away for those few moments. I was their leader and, even though I was barely conscious, I still needed to find a way to lead them through this situation. I thought, "I'm still in this. I still have to do my part for these guys. I have to fight for *them*." The power of this moment was enough to snap me back to full consciousness.

They pulled me into the vehicle and sat me up, which

forced blood into my chest cavity, helping me regain a sense of awareness. I'd lost most of the blood in my body by that point.

At that moment, I remembered the video camera that Harper and I saw in the back seat of the driver's car. This was obvious this had been some type of ambush, and we needed to detain that driver and bring him with us for questioning. My men were laser-focused on evacuating me and Harper—seconds counted at this point if we had any chance of survival. But I knew it was essential to confiscate the camera and detain the driver before we left. Doing so might prevent future attacks, and valuable intelligence might be gained from the camera footage.

I tried to get the attention of my men. I tried to tell them to detain the driver before they left, but my words weren't making sense. I could barely speak and could only muster up a word or two, not enough for them to understand what I meant. I realized it wasn't working and collapsed on the floor of the vehicle as we prepared to pull away.

At this point Daniel had a choice to make. He had examined Marlon, whose wound was shocking and the blood loss massive. I was better off, but not by much. Daniel had to make a split second decision. Who to attempt to save? He chose me. Rank had no bearing in the decision. Emotion had no bearing—remember, Marlon was beloved by these men. It was a practical decision. Medics are trained to triage patients. In this situation, I had a slightly better chance of survival. Daniel chose to get in the vehicle with me, while others tended to Marlon in the other vehicle.

At only nineteen years of age, he had a fraction of a second to make a choice that would remain with him for the rest of his life.

Regardless of the outcome of that choice, it is decisions like these that plant the seeds for moral, ethical, and spiritual turmoil in years to come. It's easy to question our actions in retrospect and make irrational assumptions about what we could've or should've done differently. It's natural to allow ourselves to focus only on the negative aspects of those decisions and take our actions out of context as the years continue to pass. It's so important to capture the details of these events, place them back into context, and remember that Daniel did everything right that day.

Talk about heroic. Daniel dove into the Bradley as the ramp was going up. This was exceedingly dangerous. The hydraulic ramp on the back of a Bradley is massive. It can sever a limb in the blink of an eye. And yet, at great risk, Daniel leapt right over the ramp to take the lead in tending to me until they could get me to a medical team. If not for his decision and quick action, I don't believe I would have made it.

For medics, this medical training is drilled into them over and over. You take care of the primary injury first. When that injury is secured, you check for secondary injuries, choking hazards, etc. And I happened to have a choking hazard that wasn't registering in my clouded brain. After Daniel applied a tourniquet to my leg, suddenly his fingers were in my mouth. He pulled out a big wad of Copenhagen chewing tobacco and tossed it aside. Even in my altered state, I was impressed. I thought, "Wow. Here's this very young soldier in the middle of a catastrophic event and he's still remembering to do his secondary checks!" Training is all well and good, but this was happening live and it was harrowing. That's the true test. Daniel was on top of everything, down to the last detail.

It was inspiring to watch all my men do their work that day under the most intense duress. It gave me an incredible sense of comfort to see them in the zone and performing brilliantly. I was proud of them, and couldn't help but feel honored to have the privilege to lead such men.

STUCK ON A TREADMILL

As the Bradley started off, I struggled to stay alert. My Kevlar helmet was uncomfortable, but I was so weak from blood loss that I couldn't even unbuckle its small plastic strap. I felt like I had given blood ten times over. I was becoming nauseous and I was on the verge of passing out. I was clearly in shock—I felt no pain at all from the wound, but what I did experience was more of an anaerobic pain. My breathing was rapid and painful, as if I were running full speed on a treadmill and couldn't stop.

I can't begin to describe the incredible and overwhelming thirst that came on. I knew from my own first aid training that you never give water to someone with a severe injury because it could complicate the surgical process. While I sat there fighting to stay conscious, I was also thinking, "How am I going to do this? I know Daniel won't give me water, but maybe I can convince him! Just a sip will be okay. Or at least a wet rag. Maybe because I'm the platoon leader he'll listen to me." In my mind, I'd prepared this solid pitch to convince him to give me a drink; but, when I opened my mouth to speak, the very best I could do, giving it all my effort, was to croak pathetically, "Water." That's it. That's all I could muster. "Water."

Daniel looked at me and a smile broke across his face. He just shook his head, "No." He knew exactly what I was trying to do. He knew that I knew better than to even ask. There was just no way. It wasn't funny to me then, but I think back on it now and have to laugh. In my recollections of that day, it's a moment that still stands out clearly: Daniel smiling, almost chuckling, shaking his head. No.

Daniel's work was done. He elevated my leg over his shoulder and sat there, placing pressure on the wound, and calmly encouraging me to stay awake. At that point, all he could do was wait. It must've been an incredibly helpless feeling for him. Our smiles from the water incident dissipated, and we both focused on making it to the aid station. Seconds before, we were laughing, but we both knew how grave the situation actually was.

A PERFECTION OF TEAMWORK

I was still reasonably alert when the Bradley came to a stop at the medical aid station at Forward Operating Base Loyalty. As the ramp began to lower, the dark interior of the vehicle flooded with light. In a moment, my eyes adjusted and I saw several people lined up, ready to bring me out to a stretcher. Their faces were grim. I wouldn't learn until eight years later that one of my West Point classmates was in this group that put me on the stretcher. He happened to be there with a different unit when the call for immediate help came in.

As they slid me out into the light of day, I noticed we were across the street from a large, concrete high-rise building that was bombed out from an earlier point in the war. On the other side, to my right, I could see soldiers busy in the operating area where they were about to take me. I wondered if I would be in the same room as Harper.

Throughout all of this, I had the comforting feeling of being in the capable hands of highly trained professionals and hoped that Harper was having this same sensation. When they moved me into the cool room, my eyes adjusted to the change of light again, but Harper wasn't there. Meanwhile, each person on that team knew exactly what to do. They worked quickly and calmly as they took off my clothes, started an IV, and began assessments. It was like they moved as one in a perfectly choreographed dance. In spite of my state, I found their precision and authority inspiring.

Behind me, someone asked, "How much blood did he lose?" Someone else answered, "I don't know. I think he lost a fucking lot!" When I heard that, I thought, "Oh crap," but in the back of my mind I was sort of laughing about it. They didn't know that I was aware of everything that was going on. I was obviously in shock, but somehow my mind was processing every detail with crystal clarity. My body wasn't cooperating though. I tried to do whatever they asked, but every effort I made seemed to create the opposite reaction. It was bizarre. It was a nearly complete disconnect of mind and body.

I was still horribly thirsty and I realized I still had a little piece of Copenhagen in my mouth. It wasn't much at all, but I was so thirsty I wanted to spit it out. There was a young female soldier who was responsible for my oxygen mask. I tried to spit the Copenhagen into the mask, but when she noticed I was trying to spit, she pulled the mask off and I spit straight up into the air and almost hit her. She jumped back and said, "Ah!" Immediately she stepped back in to put the mask back on. Again, here I was, laughing at myself, thinking, "Well that was a fail!" I felt really bad about this and actually tried to say, "I'm sorry," but couldn't get the words out.

At this point everything started to get very real. I was fighting to stay conscious, but it was harder and harder to breathe—as if I were running endless wind sprints while trying to breathe through a straw. When I tried to sit up to get a breath, they pressed me back down. Every time I sat up I felt like it was easier to breathe. They didn't understand how badly I needed to sit up and I couldn't tell them; so, with all my remaining strength, I sat up so aggressively that I ripped an IV out, which basically "exploded" my vein. I didn't feel a thing, but I did feel something when they pushed me back down. I felt like I was suffocating.

During a catastrophic injury, the body pulls blood into the chest cavity in order to protect itself. I could actually feel that happening. As all the blood crept up from my legs, they cramped up and went numb. This creeping blood sensation moved up through my quads, then they went numb. When it hit my stomach, it became even more difficult to breathe, and for the first time I understood that the injury was getting out of control. I was dying. In my thoughts, I started saying three names in rapid succession. I said, "Mom...," and my sisters' names, "Melissa, Kendra." Mom, Melissa, Kendra. Mom, Melissa, Kendra. I didn't consciously try to say their names. It literally just happened. We've all heard that when faced with death "life flashes before your eyes." I didn't have that experience, per se, but I can't help but think that the most important aspects of my life presented themselves to me at that moment: Mom, Melissa, and Kendra.

Just then, our battalion commander came in. He was a tall guy with a large, rectangular-shaped head. It's almost as if his head "floated" in from the left. He leaned down near my face and said, "Stay calm, Josh. Hang in there." If he only knew. I was so far beyond any ability to hang in there. But what else could he say? It's an incredibly helpless feeling to watch a loved one or comrade fighting for their life and not being able to do anything about it. But the fact that he was there and tried meant a lot to me. The creeping blood sensation felt like it bloomed in my chest and I knew that was it. I took my last breath, my mind whispered, "Please take care of them," and I died.

PEACEFUL AND POWERFUL

When I tell people about this experience, there's one question that everyone is most curious about. They want to know if I had an out-of-body experience.

The answer is no, I didn't. But I believe that my experience was maybe even more powerful than an out-of-body experience.

There's a lot of controversy and endless questions surrounding near-death experiences. Are they real? Are the deceased actually still conscious? Are they in a dream state? Do they experience some trick of the brain? Or is the experience absolutely real and just beyond our understanding?

In my final moment of life—in the last second, as everything literally faded to black—I experienced a peace more profound than anything I could've ever imagined. I can only describe it as a feeling of absolute surrender to something higher. There was no fear. No anxiety. No sadness or remorse. There was nothing except the feeling of a connection to something much greater than ourselves that is impossible to fully capture in words.

In our lives, most of us never really reach a point of true surrender. We might have some conscious beliefs or mental reservations or physical reservations or something else preventing us from getting there. But this surrender, in that moment, was a transition point that I could not stop. There was no need to stop it—no need at all for resistance. It was the most peaceful, powerful feeling I've ever experienced.

As it was happening, I remember thinking, "Well, here it goes. I guess this is it." There was no arguing with it or controlling it. It took away everything. Every worry, every doubt, every positive, every negative—everything became one. It was as if my spirit became part of everything, and nothing, at the same time.

The moment of my death became the most peaceful experience of my life—a thought that I would toil over greatly in the years to come.

ABOVE AND WAY BEYOND

After I flatlined, a convergence of well-timed good fortune occurred that day. It was almost as if larger forces were at work, determined not to let me go.

There was this big guy named Tipton on the medical team. He was a private first class, maybe twenty years old, and a former football player. A very strong guy. He started CPR as soon as I flatlined. Doing chest compressions is exhausting work. The compressions have to be steady, fast, and hard. If it weren't for Tipton putting those relentless compressions on my chest the entire time I was flatlined, I wouldn't be here. No question.

The FOB Loyalty medical facility was small, so the equipment was pretty basic, especially when it came to life-saving equipment. In fact, a defibrillator had been delivered and installed just that morning. They had to unwrap the plastic on the paddles to use it on me! Imagine if I had been wounded a day earlier, or if the defibrillator delivery had been delayed by a few hours.

When a patient flatlines, most physicians perform CPR and other life-saving interventions for about six minutes. After the six-minute mark, the likelihood that you'll bring a patient back is exceedingly slim. Even if you do, the extended oxygen deprivation pretty much guarantees severe brain damage. And yet, when six minutes came and went, this dedicated medical team did not let up. Tipton continued CPR, someone else continued with the defibrillation, and other medics pumped me full of atropine, epinephrine, and sodium bicarbonate through my IV.

At ten minutes, it was time to let it go and acknowledge that they'd given it their best shot. At that point, anyone would have commended them for going above and beyond. But they didn't give up. At twelve minutes, thirteen minutes, fourteen minutes, I was surely a lost cause. But they didn't give up. And then—literally against *all* odds—at fifteen minutes, someone said, "We've got a pulse!"

It was faint. But it was a pulse. And we were on the move again.

PULLING OUT ALL THE STOPS

I wasn't conscious through this next part—and some of these details weren't shared with me until years later—but while I was submerged in the deepest imaginable sleep, this amazing medical team quickly and carefully placed me on a stretcher and raced outside to a Black Hawk helicopter waiting on standby in case it was needed.

My men—my scouts—were outside waiting too. They already knew that their brother-in-arms, Marlon Harper, had died. They were expecting to hear the same news about me at any moment. When they saw us come out and realized I wasn't gone, they stepped up and said to the medical team, "He's our lieutenant. We're going to put him in that bird." They actually took the stretcher from them and loaded me up into the helicopter. It was something they felt like they needed to do themselves. Perhaps it was their attempt to take back control from the sniper who stole it from them just minutes earlier.

I'll always be very moved by the camaraderie and loyalty in that simple gesture. It's humbling to think of my guys and all of the other fine people who were so invested in my survival that day. I still get chills when I think about it.

The Black Hawk rushed me to the Green Zone where more good fortune was waiting. The surgeon there performed a vascular surgery, one that would have been perfect under normal conditions, but easily rated as somewhere above perfect given the crisis situation. Meanwhile, medics were scouring the base for soldiers with my blood match, making phone calls, dragging in whoever they could. It was so urgent that they'd sit a soldier down and pull blood straight out of their body and put it into mine. They didn't have time to test it. In the middle of a blood shortage in Baghdad, they scraped together nearly thirty units of blood. Much of it drained right out of me until the artery was fully repaired, so they had to keep it coming.

After pulling out every stop to save me, my condition stabilized. Now, they could only wait to see if I would come around. If I did, they would begin assessing the brain damage, which they assumed would be significant.

LUCKY BOY

It was the afternoon, roughly two days later, when I opened my eyes. My brain was bogged down in a foggy haze. They had me on methadone, morphine, Percocet, and probably a half-dozen other drugs. When I was finally able to focus, I found myself looking at a pretty blonde nurse in a white uniform. The room was dark, and in my fuzzy vision, she was surrounded by a hazy light. I jokingly thought to myself, "Is this Heaven?"

But apparently, I said that out loud. The nurse turned to me with a surprised look on her face. She said, "Hi!"

I said, "Hi."

She said, "Can you tell me your name?"

"Yeah. Josh Mantz."

"Do you know where you are?"

"Ummm...FOB Loyalty?"

Her jaw dropped. "No, you're in the Green Zone. But you were at FOB Loyalty when you were last conscious. Do you remember what happened?"

This was a tougher question in my state, but I was up to the task. I told her about our patrol with the humanitarian drop and how we got a call to help out another platoon under fire. Then it hit me. I had to ask, although I knew the answer. "Did Marlon Harper make it?

"No," she said. "Unfortunately he didn't."

"Yeah, I kind of thought so."

She excused herself and quickly returned with a surgeon. They were stunned that I was able to speak clearly and remember events in such great detail. There were no apparent signs of brain damage.

Within a couple of hours, they had stabilized me and put me on a Black Hawk headed to another aid station at Balad Air Base, about fifty miles north of Baghdad. One of the Black Hawk crew members tucked me in with a blanket in a tight compartment in the back of the helicopter. He was in a blacked out helmet and it was dark outside, so I couldn't see his face. He leaned down and said, "You're going to be alright, buddy." There was a steady tone in his voice that put me at ease.

That gave me a lot of comfort. Here was this person I'd never met, a fellow soldier, yet this simple act of concern reinforced the bonds of brotherhood shared by all of us in the military. It was a powerful moment, but it also let me know I was not out of the woods yet. In spite of there being no signs of brain damage, people looked worried.

When we got to Balad it was the middle of the night. They took me to a room and got me settled in. A doctor came by and looked at my chart. She looked at me. Looked at my chart again. Looked back at me. She did this one more time and shook her head. She said, "You are one lucky boy."

I smiled. "Yeah. I know."

Chapter 7

The Patient

MY MOTHER WAS MAKING A GRILLED CHEESE SANDWICH for my little sister Kendra. She was almost finished when she stopped cold. Out of the blue, she felt an overwhelming sense of dread that made her dizzy and nauseous. She had to brace herself on the table.

The sandwich started to burn, but she didn't even notice at first. Within a few minutes, the phone rang—the sound of it went through her with a bolt of fear. It was an unexplainable moment of pure premonition, an energy felt between a mother and her child half way around the world. She told me later that picking up that phone was the most frightening moment of her life. It was the Department of Defense calling to tell her that I had been critically wounded in combat, and that I likely wouldn't make it through the night.

The department made immediate arrangements for my mom and Degg to travel to Germany to visit me, even though my survival at that moment was still in doubt. If I pulled through, the plan was to transfer me to the US military hospital in Landstuhl, Germany, as soon as possible. But just as they were about to get on the plane, someone from the department called again and gave my mom a surprising update. I had come out of the surgery and was doing surprisingly well. They intended to send me back to the US within the next day or two, and recommended that she and Degg meet me at Walter Reed Hospital in Washington, DC, instead.

A few hours later, soon after arriving in Balad, I called my mom. She was emotional and her voice was shaky. I tried to sound as normal as possible. Making light of the situation, I said, "Mom, I'm good. Don't worry about it. It's just a scratch." I felt bad for her. She still hadn't quite gotten past one of the biggest scares of her life.

Once I was stable, I made the trip to Landstuhl. They performed another surgery there to close up part of my leg. Soon after, I set off on the ten-hour flight back to the US in the company of a flight surgeon, a flight nurse, and a couple of other medical people. They continued to meticulously monitor my condition. Every step of the journey—from the Green Zone, to Balad, to Landstuhl, to the US, and eventually, with a police escort no less, to Walter Reed Army Medical Center—I was given exceptional care.

I was still heavily medicated, so I continued to feel no pain at all. Still, I knew how severe my injury was. The road to recovery would be long, no doubt. I already had it in my head that I wanted to get back to Baghdad and continue the work I'd just gotten started with the scout platoon. But that wasn't going to happen anytime soon. I had to consciously shove aside the thought that it might not happen at all.

On the plane ride to DC, every passing minute didn't feel like a minute closer to home, but rather a minute further away from my men. Despite the severity of my injury, to my mind, it didn't justify my absence. I knew I had to go through this recovery, but I had a nagging heartache of lost connection and guilt—I wasn't where I knew I belonged.

From the moment we landed, every little detail was taken care of. It made me restless because it seemed like I should be doing something, though I couldn't move. It was actually strange to be taken care of like that. Normally, I was the one in control. I was the guy fixing unexpected situations. It was awkward to play a passive role, especially with everyone around me doing their work with such expert precision and thoughtfulness. All I could do was to just go along for the ride.

The staff placed me in the intensive care unit as soon as we arrived at Walter Reed. When they got me settled, they invited my parents in. They didn't know what to expect—what I would look like or how I would act or what I would say—so they were terribly worried.

My mom was relieved when she saw me, and I tried to be upbeat and keep it light.

About an hour later, my best friend Jessie Scholl and his wife Lindsey came by. We were very close growing up and my mom had called him as soon as she got the news that I'd been injured so badly. Jessie and I had been through a lot, going back to our childhood. He was in Junior ROTC with me in high school, and he was the one who called me when our friend Brett Swank had been killed in Iraq when I was still at West Point.

Mom had told me how worried Jessie had been. So, when he walked into the room, I had to rib him a little. I said, "Hey, I heard you cried when mom told you I died, you wuss!" I had him cracking up first thing. He understood. He knew it was my way of saying, "Don't worry. I'm okay."

HOPE, TRUST, AND VINDICATION

A couple of days after I arrived at Walter Reed, I got a phone call from Iraq. It was my scout platoon sergeant, Eric Smith. He said, "Hey, sir. We got him."

I didn't get it at first. I said, "What? We got who?"

"We got the cell leader responsible for the sniper attack."

This was incredible! Even better, this insurgent leader happened to be one of the top targets we'd been chasing down from the first day I'd arrived in Baghdad. He was a cunning and elusive character. I was joyous that my guys had found and detained him. The way it all unfolded was tremendously satisfying.

This insurgent sniper team came from outside our

sector, so they had no way of knowing the quality of our relationship with people in the neighborhood. Eric explained that after Marlon and I were shot, people were actually coming out of their houses to help guide the American trucks, shouting, "He went that way!" They put themselves at extreme personal risk to help capture the man who had shot, and whom they believed had killed the White Horse.

We later found out that individual community leaders who we had worked so hard to build a rapport with were the very ones who called in additional intelligence tips. What was their reason for putting their lives on the line like that? Simple. They liked us. We had become the Americans they trusted, the ones who gave them hope for a better future. We had ingrained ourselves into the life of their neighborhood, and, to some extent, we were part of that community. If they were teetering between trusting us and fearing the insurgents, that one terrible sniper shot tipped the balance. On that day, the connection and the trust shone through.

Sometime later, long after Eric's call, we were told an interesting detail about that national police chief, who had been so timid about associating with us at first. When he learned that our platoon was attacked and Marlon and I were shot, he was so angered that he flipped over his solid oak desk in his office, and then sent his entire battalion out into Baghdad to help track down the sniper. That's truly amazing. That just does *not* happen.

The phone call from Eric left me with a phenomenal feeling of satisfaction. Now I knew that our counterinsurgency strategies were solid and the relationships we had worked exhaustively to build were paying off. I was heartbroken to lose Marlon Harper to get to that moment, and I never would have willingly volunteered to go through my own harrowing ordeal, but this was success, hard won. If my team maintained that momentum, which I knew they would, it would progressively increase the safety of the entire area for everyone.

The idea of returning to Baghdad had already been circling in my mind. Eric's phone call was all I needed to fully ignite the idea. I might not have consciously seized on the thought that day, but my path was set. I was going back to Baghdad.

TAKING LEAVE IN THE MOUNTAINS

I had one nightmare during my four-month stay at Walter Reed.

I was walking down a street in Baghdad at night. I was alone and I could hear my own footsteps. There was a puddle in the dimly lit street. I stepped into the puddle, heard my foot slosh in the water, then took a second step into the puddle. The moment I knew it was a booby trap it was too late. *Boom!* I woke up with a violent start, scared and hyperventilating.

Another time when Jessie was visiting, it was late, I was

tired and half asleep. He got up to leave and I said, "All right, man. Just make sure you secure the road before you head back." I was serious, giving him operational orders. He said, "What the hell are you talking about?" Once I broke out of the delirium, we just laughed it off. Obviously my mind was not completely home yet. But I was fortunate. These two instances were fairly mild and I otherwise didn't show any signs of the anxiety, jumpiness, or recurring nightmares that are common to the post-traumatic state.

I did have one scare, though, where I thought it was all about to cave in on me.

After a few weeks, I became stable enough for a thirty-day convalescent leave. My doctors believed that I was coming along well and I could spend some of my recovery period at home. The idea is that you tend to acclimate and heal faster when you're with your family and away from the hospital, where the environment can be stressful at times. By that point, I had been taking frequent trips outside the hospital. I would head down to the National Mall in DC and walk around the monuments at night. It was an eerie feeling, but reassuring to think of the heroic stories of past generations. In many ways, spending time there helped me work up the strength to go back. In the company of those monuments, my desire to go back wasn't something heroic or crazy or special. It was a necessity.

Later, I started going to the gym where I walked the track as fast as I could, sometimes even jogging. Of course, my mind was set on Baghdad. I was also feeling the pressure of time running out. My unit was set to come back in January. In order to get in enough time over there to make it worthwhile, I had to get back as soon as possible.

When I was home with my family in Pennsylvania, I started hiking in the Appalachian Mountains, pushing myself on steep trails to get stronger. I was still taking full doses of methadone and Percocet. Then, one day, I decided I didn't need the methadone anymore. I stopped taking it. It didn't occur to me to tell one of my doctors. After all, I was feeling so much better. No problem! Except it was a huge problem.

Within just a couple of days, I started waking up from horrible nightmares, night sweats, and panics. It really threw me. I thought, *This is it. This must be post-traumatic stress. This can't be me.* I finally talked to a nurse about it and we put it together. I'd had no idea that you couldn't just stop taking methadone. You have to carefully wean yourself off under the supervision of a doctor. I knew it was a powerful narcotic, but I didn't think I was addicted to it.

After a few days, the symptoms of withdrawal leveled off. It was a relief to know that waking up in a panic, drenched in sweat every night, was not my new normal. But it did give me a first-hand glimpse into what life might be like for people who are recovering from deep emotional trauma and addiction. This frightening episode was quickly behind me, but I would think of it often in coming years as I came to better understand the challenges that so many people face as they struggle to recover from trauma.

TAKING CARE OF THEIR OWN

Around the time of the troop surge to Baghdad, the Department of Defense established the Warrior Transition Unit in response to the sharp spike in casualties happening with the war in Iraq. The sheer number of injured soldiers was overwhelming, but the true core of the problem was the complex nature of the injuries. On one hand, you had some of the most severe behavioral health conditions, such as major depressive disorders and severe anxiety, in addition to post-traumatic stress. Any one of those issues would be hard enough for any returning soldier to deal with. Most of these issues were complicated by severe physical injuries, including the all-too-common traumatic brain injury caused by roadside bombs.

Some of these soldiers would have several medical appointments every day, ranging from various behavioral health sessions to wound care to complex physical therapy. The Warrior Transition Unit was designed to rehabilitate and nurture these patients with a deliberate, comprehensive approach that's typically outside the scope of traditional caregivers.

The original purpose of WTU was to either help soldiers heal to the point where they could return to full duty in the military, or—more commonly—to help them transition out of the military and find successful employment in the civilian world. The Department of Defense didn't want to just throw these people out into the civilian population. They did everything they could to set them up for success.

Soldiers in this unit have only one mission: to heal. That's it. They're not assigned to other military tasks. Their exclusive focus is to attend medical appointments, put in the time with physical therapy, and heal. Their overarching purpose is to set themselves up, using all the available resources, to transition back into active duty or out of the service.

The first of these units was created at Walter Reed, and that's the one I was assigned to. To be honest, I didn't have much use for it. Ironically, I would be assigned to lead one of these units a few years later. But, in 2007, my laser focus on getting back to Baghdad meant that I was taking charge of my own rehab by constantly working out and staying busy. I took advantage of the freedom and the time to heal offered by WTU. Between that and the excellent care I received at Walter Reed, I had everything I needed to get myself in shape to rejoin my unit, my team, and my mission.

A CAUTIOUS BLESSING

I didn't need any further motivation to return to Baghdad, but I got one. And it was powerful. My platoon sergeant, Eric Smith, was hit by an IED.

Fortunately, Eric survived, but he was evacuated out of

theater and went straight back to Fort Hood, Texas. The nature of his injuries guaranteed that he would not return to Baghdad. When I heard that, my own return to Baghdad suddenly became hugely important.

Eric was the senior noncommissioned officer of the scout platoon. That meant that when Marlon Harper died and I was sent back home to Walter Reed, Eric became their sole leader. Normally, Eric was my direct counterpart. I was the platoon leader, and he was the platoon sergeant. In the simplest of terms, the platoon leader strategically guides the platoon, while the platoon sergeant drives the execution of missions and tasks.

Eric was a phenomenal leader and embodied the non-commissioned officer role in every sense of the word. He was an Army Ranger and had a ton of experience under his belt. He held his men to high standards. After a patrol, it wasn't uncommon to find Eric meticulously cleaning every weapon, every bullet, every piece of gear, and every vehicle. He was a master of attention to detail, and did everything in his power to eliminate Murphy's Law, his all-out effort to protect his men. Some of the young soldiers hated him for it. But later in their careers, as they themselves assumed leadership roles, they saw the value in Eric's discipline. Most modeled themselves after him and are still serving as leaders in our Armed Forces today.

In our absence, he was running the entire platoon by himself. Now, he was gone too, so the platoon had no senior leader. During the most complex and intense period of the war, the people driving the scene were young staff sergeants. I knew they were highly capable, first-rate soldiers, but I also knew they needed leadership. Just as important, they needed a morale boost. I knew what it would mean to them if I landed at FOB Rustamiyah and stepped back in to guide their mission. That was the extra boost that focused me even more on getting back.

From the moment I arrived home, virtually everyone advised me to forget this idea of returning to Baghdad. When I first met my surgeon at Walter Reed, I asked him how soon he thought it might be until I was ready to go back to Baghdad. He shook his head and said, "Son, you're not going to be going anywhere for quite a while." The way he said it, I knew what he really meant was that it was very unlikely I'd ever go back. But he had no idea that he was talking to—in the most literal sense—a man on a mission.

After a couple of months of steady improvement, that same surgeon gave me permission to return. Sort of. It wasn't a full blown approval. It was a half blessing—a cautious blessing. And I know he wouldn't have even given me that much if I'd been completely honest about my physical condition. All of my medical testing checked out. But when asked if I could run, if I was physically fit, my answer was less than truthful. I said, "Oh yeah. I'm running around the track. I'm doing really well." That was stretching it a bit.

TWO PURPLE HEARTS

But the stretch worked. I was released from Walter Reed and sent to Fort Hood where I started a deployment process. This included a lot of administrative details like power of attorney, a will, and a medical verification. But there was one looming obstacle: a physical fitness test. I didn't know how in the world I would do it, but I was determined to pass.

When I arrived at Fort Hood, Eric Smith picked me up at the airport and we went out to dinner to catch up. Even though we'd spoken when he called to tell me they'd detained the sniper cell leader after Marlon and I were shot, this was really our first chance to talk at length. And it was a hard conversation. We were both close to Marlon, but Eric took Marlon's death especially hard. They'd been very close, professionally and personally, for many years.

When Marlon and I were suddenly pulled out of the scene, Eric continued to lead the platoon. He was more than capable, but our loss had been traumatic. Tending to Marlon's body, helping clean my blood out of the Bradley, then having to carry on only a few hours later and take over my responsibilities had clearly weighed heavily on him.

Eric filled me in on a lot of details of what had been going on since that day. Insurgent attacks were on the rise and it was getting ugly in Baghdad. He was just as driven as I was to return to our team, but we both knew that it wasn't going to happen, and he took that hard. A few days later, they had a Purple Heart ceremony at the base and Eric and I received our Purple Hearts together. It was bittersweet. We both would have given anything to have Marlon by our side. Moreover, Eric knew that I was going back in a few days, and that he couldn't. He would've given anything to go with me. He knew I had to go back, but I felt guilty leaving him. He was my counterpart throughout the war, and I didn't want to leave him alone. I knew how emotionally difficult it was to stay behind.

DODGING THE VERIFICATION

The morning of my physical fitness test I woke up wondering, *How in the hell am I going to do this?*

I knew that in order to pass the test, I would have to run two miles within a time limit. I knew I would be cutting it close. I was running again, but wasn't completely sure I'd be able to meet the time limit, and it was causing a lot of anxiety. I didn't want a two-mile run to stop me after I'd come so far. I knew I just needed another week or two and I'd be fine, but the date of the test was fixed. When asked if I was ready, I bent the truth a bit and said, "I'm good. Let's just get me on that plane." Because we were under a time crunch, they took me at my word, making an exception to policy—I didn't have to test.

So the fitness test didn't pose a problem. The medical verification, however, was another story. Unexpectedly, that one almost tripped me up.

At that point, my wound was just barely healed. I was pulling staples out of my leg with a Leatherman multi-tool right before I left Walter Reed, so I should have suspected that someone might have questioned my readiness.

They do medical verifications en masse on certain days of the week. It's a very structured process where you go from one station to the next. I got to one particular station and I had my medical records in my hand. They were as thick as an encyclopedia by now. I handed it to the physician's assistant who was making the final decision. She took one look at my records and said, "You can't go. There's no way we're letting you on that plane." I tried to talk her out of it, I nearly pleaded, but she wouldn't budge. For now, it was over.

I stepped away, almost in a panic, and surveyed the situation. I realized there were a few of these people who were making the final decisions. They weren't using computer records, they only went by the printed medical records—so I took a chance. I folded all the documentation that related to my injury and slipped it in the side of my pants. Then I got in a different line and hoped that that first physician's assistant wouldn't spot me. No problem—I sailed right through. The physician's assistant at the head of that line waved me through and I was confirmed to leave two days later.

A LUCKY COIN

Getting on the plane to begin the return trip to Baghdad

was an eerie feeling. In truth, I knew I was still kind of a mess, but I was hyped about going back. There was a part of me that wasn't ready for it, wondering what the hell I was doing. But I had a strong selfless feeling about doing it for my men. That's where all my drive came from.—at least I thought it did at the time. I believed that I had to do it, regardless of how I felt physically. On some level, I was fluctuating back and forth, but I was also firm in my resolve. There was something much deeper driving me, but I couldn't put my finger on what it was. So I just forced myself to push through it.

I was concerned about my family too. I knew this was hard on my mom and little sister Kendra, especially. It wouldn't really hit me until some years later how little thought I had given to their pleas for me to stay. I knew they understood why I wanted to return, and I knew that they supported me—but I was void of empathy and took their support at face value, not allowing myself to look deeper into their emotional state. I was so self-consumed in my focus on getting back to my men that I didn't bother to take measure of the roller coaster ride of deep trauma they had just been through. They had to endure my violent death, my survival, my recovery, and now my overwhelming desire to flee from them to a cauldron of violence halfway around the world. I'm sure they were terrified, but all I could see was the road ahead.

Even though I knew what I was doing, I also had a troubled mind and it was apparently showing through. I was at the Atlanta airport, changing planes and headed for Bangor, Maine, where I would catch another plane to Europe, and ultimately Iraq. I was in uniform, sitting in a corner away from everyone else at the terminal. I was feeling a bit emotional. Though I wasn't crying, I was in deep thought. A look of distress must have been heavy on my face, because a man with an English accent suddenly approached me and asked, "Excuse me, are you going overseas?"

"Yes, I am."

He reached into his pocket, pulled out a coin, and handed it to me. He said, "This is an old English guinea. I've carried it in my pocket since I was a kid. It's kind of a good luck charm and I want you to have it." He handed it to me. "Stay safe over there." That was it. Then he was gone.

I guess he picked up on my energy and was moved to do this generous thing. It was beautiful. It lifted me right up and got me focused again. To this day, I still have that guinea. He had also given me his email address, but it was illegible; I've never been able to contact him to thank him for helping me smooth out my troubled mind that night. I doubt he'd ever understand the huge impact his genuine act of human kindness had on me that day. It was almost surreal that he'd appeared in my life when he did. Almost angelic.

Three more long flights and I finally touched down. Stepping out on the tarmac, I couldn't help but think back on my first day in Baghdad. I was so green then. Only a few months had passed, but it seemed like a lifetime ago. I was a completely different person. Now, here I was boarding a Black Hawk at sunset. Just a few of minutes later the helicopter banked and I could see the lights of FOB Rustamiyah. I was excited. I was back. It was exactly where I needed to be, and I'd probably never felt more "at home" than that very moment.

THE PERMANENT BOND

As the Black Hawk came around to land, I looked directly down to where the scouts' barracks were. They had finished their patrol for the day and some were outside playing volleyball. When I stepped off the helicopter, I headed straight over to the barracks. As I approached, one of the guys spotted me and yelled, "No way, LT is back!" He ran into the barracks and returned seconds later with the whole platoon following him. All forty men greeted me at once and peppered me with questions: "What happened?" "What was it like?" "How are you still alive?" "Can't believe you're back!" It was excitement through the roof.

The level of trust between an officer and his soldiers is incredibly difficult to build with depth. The only way to do it is if your men truly believe you'd do anything required to support them, that you'd lay down your life for them, just as much as they would for you. That's a hard thing to do. Even in combat there tends to be a bit of a barrier between officers and enlisted members. In many cases, this happens because the officers make the decisions, and sometimes that involves making hard choices that isolate certain people. You make decisions all the time that people don't always agree with. Sometimes you're wrong and sometimes you're right. In this environment, being wrong can be fatal. That's a hard thing to navigate. It can compromise trust. But you have to make the best decision you can with the information you have available, take other people's input into strong consideration, and do your very best to explain the "why" behind your actions in order to gain their support.

Before I was injured, I thought I had an incredible level of rapport and trust and respect with the team. But it was on a completely new level after the shooting. Part of this might've been because I tried to save Marlon when we were shot. I'd tried to perform first aid on him until I collapsed. But it was also because I came back to them—they all knew that it was nearly impossible and not required. Those two things put a permanent bond in place between us that we share to this day. It was never about me. It was always about them and the unit and the unbreakable relationships we shared with each other.

After spending time with the scouts, I went to battalion headquarters and ran into Jeff Morris, my former company commander, who is still a great friend of mine. He was thrilled to see me. He wanted to know everything about what had been happening with me. He was especially interested in my injury. You have to understand, from the point of view of an infantry guy, surviving this level of injury is kind of epic.

In his deep, commanding voice, he said, "Let me see your scars." He wasn't kidding. He didn't care that we were standing outside, right in front of headquarters. He said, "Drop 'em. I want to see the scars." There I was, with my pants around my ankles (no underwear), and Jeff is down on his knees with a flashlight getting a good look at the impressive mess of scars. Then, around the corner walks this young private who stops short when he sees us. He had the look of a deer caught in headlights and had no idea what to do. Jeff says to him, "You need to come over here and see this, son!" That was Jeff's sense of humor. The private just scampered away, and we cracked up.

VALIDATION

Soon after I got back, there was another visit I had to make. I found out that the trauma team that worked so hard on me—literally brought me back from death—was still deployed. I checked with their base and went out to see them. They couldn't believe it when I walked in and said hello.

What they found to be even more surprising was that I remembered everything in so much detail. I remembered their faces, remembered what they said and where around the table each of them was standing while they worked on me. They were amazed. I'd been in full-blown shock—they assumed I wouldn't remember any of it. I even recognized the female soldier who was almost hit in the face with the little wad of Copenhagen when I spit it out. I'll admit, I was still quite embarrassed by that, and I just couldn't bring myself to bring it up. I hoped she had forgotten.

Connecting with these people again was important to me. Most of them were in their teens or early twenties, and they had pulled off what seemed to be a miracle. They had even taken their medical record of the incident and hung it on the wall. They told me they had put it there as a reminder of the high level of accomplishment they were capable of when the moment called for it.

The opportunity to meet them again and thank them for what they did was one of the most powerful experiences of my life.

WE NEVER QUIT

So, how *does* a guy have the astounding good fortune to survive fifteen minutes of flatlining and end up with no brain damage? That's a question I'm frequently asked, and, thanks to a BBC journalist, I have an answer. This journalist went to the trouble to set up a three-way interview between herself, brigade surgeon Dr. Dave DeBlasio, and me. When asked to explain this apparent miracle, Dave explained that several things came into play that afternoon. First, they were able to begin CPR immediately after I flatlined. They also immediately started administering life-saving drugs. After that, sheer luck was a big factor. Somehow, all their efforts kept just enough blood with just enough oxygen circulating through my brain. Dave added that it also helps a lot to have a patient who's in top physical condition, as I was.

On the day I visited the medical team, I had a chance to ask Dave another question I'd wondered about. Why did they keep working on me after I'd flatlined for over six minutes? Why did they continue for so long after that typical cutoff point? Dave looked me in the eye and, without hesitation, simply said, "We never quit."

At some point, of course, they would have had to quit, but he told me that with someone who's young and in top physical condition, you just keep at it. He said, "You were alive when you came to us and flatlined on our table. We refused to let you go." It was truly an effort of gritty perseverance from a trauma team you could hold up beside the very best in the world. That level of dedication to their mission is the reason I'm still here. They never quit. I'm forever grateful for that.

Dave DeBlasio's trauma team handled over three hundred severe trauma cases during their deployment to Baghdad. This means that on a near-daily basis they were charged with the responsibility of saving someone's life. For some, they were successful. For others, they were not. This is an enormously stressful career that is laden with moral injury and inherent trauma. Even though they themselves weren't physically wounded, the traumatic impact on the mind is the same, if not worse. Trauma units and ER teams don't often get to see the results of their work. In a case like mine, they got a faint pulse back and sent me to the next echelon of care, not knowing if I would live or die, and having to go off of faith alone that they did everything they could to bring me back. Rarely do patients like me get the opportunity to come back and thank them for their work. This endless effect of "not knowing" can leave the human mind in turmoil, constantly second-guessing your actions. Thanking them wasn't just therapeutic for me—it was therapeutic for them.

A RUMBLE OF THUNDER

I soon found out that my platoon's deployment had changed dramatically. Eric had braced me for that, but it was eye-opening to see it firsthand. A lot of the faces had changed. They'd gotten hit pretty hard and the stress on the unit was obvious. All of the units were now living out in the sector for several days, sometimes several weeks at a time. That's great from a counterinsurgency standpoint, but they were getting worn down and you could see on their faces that it was taking a toll.

While I was at Walter Reed, my battalion commander had stopped in to see me while he was on leave in Washington, DC. I told him I was feeling good and wanted to return as soon as possible. He put his hand on my shoulder and said, "Take your time, Josh. You know we'll be there. We want you to heal. That's all we're concerned about right now." I think what he was probably saying was, "We want you to be well. If you can't come back that's okay." But what I heard was a bit different. To my mind, he was saying that the door was open and they would be ready when I was.

It's true, I was welcomed back with opened arms. I'd assumed that I'd take over the leadership of the platoon again, but my battalion commander had a different plan for me. He asked me to be an executive officer for one of the companies. This is an important role, but it's not the same thing as leading a platoon in counterinsurgency efforts. Not even close.

i wasn't going to argue. He explained his justification and I accepted it. One of my colleagues ended up taking over the scout platoon; he felt really bad that he would lead instead of me. It was awkward, but I didn't begrudge him at all. He was an excellent officer and he deserved the assignment. I knew the scouts would be in great hands under his leadership.

In retrospect, I believe the battalion commander did this deliberately; he sensed that I might not be completely ready to be in a forward position out on the increasingly difficult streets of Baghdad. I can't say for sure that that's what he was thinking, but I do believe it was a good move.

I say that because of what happened when I went out on my first patrol in the executive officer position. Compared to what I had been doing before I was shot, this "patrol" was nothing more than a drive from the main base out to the middle of the sector where the unit was living at the time. That doesn't mean it wasn't dangerous—there was always the threat of IEDs—but this was nothing like the level of danger I'd lived with daily during my first few months in Iraq.

I was riding in the front seat of an Abrams tank with the most experienced tank commander in the battalion driving. I was in good hands. At the gate to the base, he paused to go through the standard procedure of calling up the start of our patrol on the radio, giving our destination and the number of soldiers going with us. When he finished and we started moving into the sector, I immediately had this sinking, sick feeling in my stomach. I just totally collapsed into myself, basically frozen. The tank commander tried to talk to me, but all I could manage to get out were tight, one-word responses. I don't believe this was technically a panic attack—I was still functional—but it might have been something like that. It was a crippling feeling of intense anxiety. At that moment, my one relief was that I was not leading a team on an actual patrol. It could've compromised them.

I had similar reactions on the next couple of patrols, and then it got better. I didn't realize that this was a classic response to trauma. In order to function every day in a combat zone, you have to develop this feeling of being almost invincible. You know you're not invincible, but you develop this attitude in order to function in an environment where you have to disregard a lot of things that are threatening and dangerous. When I got shot, that sense of invincibility was snatched away. When I went out on that first patrol, it was like I was missing a vital piece of armor, and my body and mind were "frozen" in place out of fear. What made it worse was that I didn't understand any of this then. I couldn't articulate it until years later. When we hit the streets on that patrol, I was utterly naked and vulnerable and didn't even know it. I couldn't make sense of it. I didn't talk with anyone about it. I toughed it out—I suppressed it, jamming it down deep inside until I felt like it was gone. But of course it wasn't. When you hear those first rumblings of an approaching thunder storm, you can ignore them, but that storm is still going to roll through. It is going to come. "Thou need not swerve the bullet" didn't have the same bravado attached to it any longer.

IF I JUST KEEP PUSHING

Fortunately, I wasn't going out into the sector as much as I would have been as leader of the scout platoon. In some ways, I think I was subconsciously (maybe even consciously) avoiding it. I was still out in the sector, but I was driving more of the administrative side of the combat effort. Occasionally I would go out on a patrol, but it was pretty rare. We were preparing to redeploy, which requires a major logistical effort in accounting for all the equipment in the entire company—thousands of pieces of equipment. This huge job was made even larger because the team had been in combat for so long that it was very disorganized; there were a lot of repairs to be made.

I threw myself into this organizational job like it was the most important mission on earth. I obsessively approached tasks to the point of perfection. Working straight through without sleep for forty-eight hours, seventy-two hours—even ninety-six hours seemed reasonable. That level of dedication was completely unnecessary, of course, but it was an ideal way to avoid processing deep-seeded feelings of shame and guilt that were quietly starting to creep in. I was suppressing and compartmentalizing at a championship level.

During all this I didn't recognize that anything was off or wrong. I was trying to push through these strange feelings, thinking that surely, if I just keep pushing, I'd get my head back into the game and everything would be alright again. The obsessive work allowed me to live outside myself and focus on a million mundane details instead of the underlying issues. But back then, I didn't even know I *had* underlying issues. The addiction to work and overachieving concealed the underlying guilt that was quietly infecting my soul like a deadly cancer.

As we approached the end of our unit's deployment, I began to dread it. It wasn't that I didn't want to return home. I wasn't opposed to it. But I had a strong reservation—this huge, empty feeling when I thought about going back. It had nothing to do with some kind of lust for combat. It had nothing to do with violence or anything like that. I think a lot of people assume that soldiers become hard-core warriors who are addicted to firefights and storming through buildings. That was never, ever me. Nor was it the case for the large majority of people I interacted with in the military.

If anything, I was hooked on the pace and intensity of the environment. It felt like it was exactly where I was supposed to be and that everything made sense again. The extreme pace made it easy to suppress my underlying emotions, making it easy to stay distracted. Why *would* I want to leave all that?

But, when January came it was time to go. I had every expectation that I would be back within a couple of years. I was fully aware of that. I felt more than ready for it—or so I thought.

Chapter 8

The Speaker

"HE WAS A GREAT, GREAT PERSON. HE DIED DOING WHAT he loved."

That's how Marlon Harper's spouse described her husband in a newspaper interview shortly after his death. He dearly loved his family—she and their three young children—but he was also driven by a deep sense of selflessness toward others that compelled him to serve.

Shortly after my unit returned from Iraq to Fort Hood, Eric Smith and I got a chance to visit her. Eric was a close friend of Marlon and his family, but even so, she was reluctant to meet with us at first. We caught her at a time when she was still quite distraught, and she questioned whether she was ready to have such a difficult conversation. We wanted to respect her healing process, but we also considered her part of the family and asked her if we could meet. Eventually she was willing to sit down and talk with us about the details of Marlon's last day.

I was apprehensive about meeting her because Marlon and I had been hit by the same bullet. He died and I lived. I was nervous that she might have some resentment about that. If one of us had to die, why Marlon? Why not me? I had no answer for that. I was willing to face up to that if I had to because I hoped that, by sharing what I remembered, I could give her a sense of peace or at least ease her mind in some way.

I was surprised to find that she'd initially been misinformed about how Marlon died. It was nearly a full year later and she still hadn't been informed of the correct details. She thought he was hit by an IED and she feared that his final moments were spent in great pain. On this one point, at least, I could give her some comfort. I struggled to find the words, so I started by telling her how Marlon looked. In that split second after we were hit, my focus locked onto his face just before he fell to the ground. I saw only what could be described as a look of acceptance in his eyes. There was no fear. No pain. He looked calm. I told her about Marlon's premonition.

I knew he was in no pain because I felt no pain. I was conscious, but he was knocked out almost immediately. Because of the severity of the wound, I could convincingly explain that to her. I also talked about my own train of thoughts as I died, just a few minutes later. Those thoughts were of my family, and I felt certain that Marlon's final fleeting thoughts were focused on her and their young son and twin daughters.

This was difficult for her to hear, but knowing that Marlon hadn't suffered seemed to bring some comfort. It was a deeply emotional moment for all three of us. Moreover, being able to discuss the overwhelming sense of surrender and peace at the moment of transition brought a powerful spiritual component to the conversation that seemed to give all of us strength.

After I went home that night and reflected on our conversation, I started to feel a sense of responsibility to share this experience of surrender with others. I came to realize that it might resonate far beyond the small circle of the three of us grieving together that day. I didn't know what the purpose of my second life was, but I felt this drive deep inside to convey that rare moment in time. It seemed to have a power that went far beyond me. A power that could potentially help others find a sense of peace in the wake of life's most traumatic events.

DON'T GET COMFORTABLE

The personnel in a unit tend to disperse after deployments are over. Soldiers go on to other assignments, and that's what happened to me shortly after I returned to Fort Hood.

My next stop was the Captain's Career Course at Fort Benning, Georgia. It was an extensive professional training program and another rewarding experience for me. When that finished up a couple of months later, I wound up in

Fort Riley, Kansas, assigned to the division headquarters battalion. We were expected to deploy to either Iraq or Afghanistan. But as I would soon learn, my unique experience was going to take me to unexpected places and shape my life in ways I couldn't begin to imagine.

The division headquarters had close to eighteen thousand soldiers, so you can imagine how massive the administrative staff was. My battalion commander and I, a new captain there, were headed to a meeting one day, when we ran into one of the deputy commanders of the organization, Brigadier General Ricky Gibbs, who stopped us short. He was a gruff guy with an intense personality and was well known for his tactical expertise. He looked at me, and coldly said, "Who are you?" I introduced myself, and he said, "All right, good," and just kept going. It was kind of an odd exchange, but I didn't think much of it.

Later, the battalion commander was in a meeting with that General and told him about my sniper incident. Apparently he was intrigued. No doubt, it's an inspiring story of resilience in the face of fatal odds—not on my part, but more because of the medical team, the expert vascular surgeon, the scout platoon, everyone who gave blood, and the countless others who pitched in with the urgent support I needed to cross back over from death to life. The General sent for me to interview for the position of his aide-de-camp. This was *not* a position I wanted. My perception of an aide-de-camp at that time was someone who fetches coffee, kisses ass, and does it as a career move. Obviously I couldn't say no to the interview, but the battalion commander encouraged me, assuring me that if I got the job it would be an incredible experience. I found that hard to believe, but I tried to stay open-minded.

I went up to the General's office and took the interview. There wasn't much to it. About ten minutes in, he asked, "So what do you think about being an aide?" I told him how much I appreciated being considered for the position, it meant a lot to me, and I was humbled (a stretch of the truth, but not much). "But frankly, sir," I said, "You as an infantry officer yourself, I'm sure you'll understand this. I'm about to take a company into combat and that's what I feel I should be doing. I feel like I don't have a choice. I have to take the infantry company." As I was saying this, he slowly sat back in his chair, crossed his arms, and smiled. He said, "Okay. Don't get comfortable." I wasn't sure what to make of that comment, so I just matched his smile, and said, "Yes, sir."

The next morning he called to tell me I was his new aide-de-camp.

Fortunately, my battalion commander was right. It was an incredible experience. A couple of days later, the General explained why he had chosen me for the job. He said, "I'm not looking for somebody who kisses ass and does whatever I say. I need somebody who can be my eyes and ears and tell me what I *need* to know, not what I *want* to know. I need somebody who's connected and has a solid perspective, and who's a strong leader. More importantly, this is going to be a strategic level education for you—a graduate level education, just by doing this job. You're going to see how the Department of Defense works from the very top, all the way down." Within a few days I could see that it was going to be a phenomenal experience. Like anything, it's all what you make of it.

Of course, I hit it just like everything else I do: full steam. And believe it or not, I found it to be even more intense than combat in many ways. That's because an aide is essentially living the General's life, and staying several steps ahead at all times. The learning curve is incredibly steep, but the perspective you gain is unparalleled. That experience would influence the way I think for the rest of my life—to think with a broader perspective and understand what's truly important while staying connected at multiple levels.

Six months in, the job was unbelievably demanding and stressful, but I was enjoying it enormously. I was preparing to deploy with the General and division headquarters to Iraq and was looking forward to an amazing experience developmentally. Then disaster struck. I had a flare-up of Crohn's disease.

I was diagnosed with Crohn's disease about a year after I graduated West Point. During the officer basic course at Fort Benning, I was floored for an entire weekend with extreme fatigue. I felt like I'd been run over by a bulldozer.

With that first flare-up, I laid in bed for two days and lost sixteen pounds. I had no idea why. Up until then, I was in the best shape of my life. I was a marathon runner, but now I could barely get around. A few weeks later, a gastro-enterologist gave me the Crohn's diagnosis. He said it was one of the most definitive cases he'd ever seen. He told me, "With Crohn's, you can't go to ranger school, you can't go to airborne school, you can't stay in the infantry, and you should probably get out of the military all together."

This was crushing news. Everything I'd worked for was falling apart in front of my eyes and my military career appeared to be over before it'd even started. I took it in. I didn't say much to the doctor. I walked out of his office and took the round of prednisone steroids he gave me. I threw the rest of the medications in the trash and immediately started running the river walk in Columbus, Georgia. I ran twenty miles just to clear my mind—almost a full marathon on a whim, fueled by anger.

By the time I got home that day I had a plan. I committed myself to learning everything I possibly could about the disease and did everything I could to manage it holistically without medication.

Crohn's disease is an immune disorder that impacts the intestinal tract and the digestive system. Basically, your immune system attacks itself and creates embedded scars in the lining of your intestines. In my case, the worst symptoms were bowel obstructions, but I also had severe pain and fatigue. If you have a chemical compound and you pull one element out of that compound, the whole thing falls apart. With Crohn's, that's what it feels like with your entire body—as if something is missing and the whole thing falls apart. It was brutal.

To save my career I changed my life. I read every book I could find about Crohn's. I reduced stress as much as I could. I completely changed my diet and rarely wavered. And it worked. I went through my deployment to Iraq with no issues. Even when I was shot, there was no Crohn's response. When I was recovering at Walter Reed, I actually went to a gastroenterologist and asked him to reverse my diagnosis. I had gone so long without any symptoms that I was convinced I was misdiagnosed. This was really important because it was keeping me from ranger school. I snuck into airborne school when I was at Fort Benning. After pulling some stuff out of my records, I was able to get by on that one, but there was no way to sneak into ranger school.

When my symptoms flared back up unexpectedly, I had to go on a significant round of prednisone to suppress it. I probably could have deployed, but the General and I talked about it and we thought that it made sense that I stayed back. One of the hardest things that I've ever had to do was watch that unit pull out of the base on the way to Iraq and not go with them.

The old cliché about one door closing and another

opening had been true for me all my life. And once again, that's exactly what happened. All three generals who had been stationed at the base shipped out with the deployment. They were replaced with Brigadier General David Petersen, who was covering down on an organization of nearly eighteen thousand people. So, where you'd normally have multiple generals, a chief of staff, and a robust division headquarters element, all of that was replaced by a small civilian component of staff members with General Petersen at the top, me as his aide, and Colonel Kevin Brown as the Garrison Commander. Out of necessity, I became an integral part of that team as we set out to take on some of the most complex challenges facing the organization.

BACK TO THE MESS HALL

At the beginning of the war in Iraq there was a powerful patriotic feeling in the country, and one of the benefits was a surge of blood donations to help the war effort. But over the years, that patriotic fervor slacked off and blood donations dropped too. By the end of the decade the supply was at a record low while the demand was higher than ever. So, in 2009, a staff sergeant I had met while I was at Walter Reed asked me to come to West Point and speak to the cadets about giving blood. He was working for the Army Blood Program which delivers all donations straight to Iraq and Afghanistan to support wounded soldiers on the battlefield.

He didn't want a full-blown speaking engagement, just a five-minute talk to share details about the sniper attack, my death, and recovery, with emphasis on the enormous amount of blood that was required to keep me alive. The blood situation on the day I was shot is just one of many things I can point to and say, "If not for that, I wouldn't be here."

The Academy campus is beautiful and I had many memories there, so I was looking forward to this return, although I knew I would be facing a tough crowd. The mess hall is huge. All four thousand cadets march in for a brief lunch period that's interrupted for announcements and sometimes a guest is introduced. You really get tired of having to stop eating for announcements when your time is limited. I've seen senators, vice-presidents, and four-star generals introduced to a fairly glum reception.

I was up on the platform in the mess hall and everyone had to pause for announcements, then I was introduced. I launched right into it, quickly recounting my experience of getting shot, flatlining, and coming back to life thanks to the brilliant efforts of the medical team. But all that would have been for nothing if they hadn't been able to round up enough blood donors on the fly while I was in surgery. I told them I'd been in their shoes not so long ago, struggling to come up with some way I might help our men and women over there. I said, "Guys, I know how hard it is. I know how busy you are. But if you want to do something right now, today, that will directly impact what's happening in Iraq and Afghanistan, then take an hour of your time to give blood. I'm living proof that it'll make a huge difference."

That was the first time I'd been asked to speak like that, to essentially leverage my experience for a positive outcome. And it was wildly successful. After I left, blood donations at West Point spiked up to near-record levels. That was huge for us to see and very gratifying. But more importantly, it was the first time that it really sunk in how this story could be a positive vehicle for change.

ONE ON ONE

Shortly after that trip to West Point, I had another experience tied to the speaking—another epiphany that showed me that there was something much more powerful to this than just a story.

By this time, the Department of Defense had come to recognize the deep emotional consequences of combat—for soldiers *and* their families. One group was called Survivor Outreach Services (SOS), which the Department created as a way to support family members of fallen soldiers. It's turned into an extensive network of spouses, children, and parents who have lost a loved one in combat.

On the spur of the moment, I was asked to speak at an SOS gathering at Fort Riley. Bonnie Carrol, the founder of an organization called TAPS (Tragedy Assistance Program for Survivors), hosted the event. Bonnie personally experienced a devastating loss when her husband, a general officer, was tragically killed in a plane crash in 1992. She's since leveraged that experience to do incredible work in helping others recover from similar situations. They were having a two-day session for well over a hundred surviving family members. These families would have a chance to meet each other, one-on-one, to share their experiences, and were offered expert guidance in navigating the grief and healing process.

With very little notice, I was asked to speak to this group for just ten minutes or so. I was given no guidance about what to say, but they thought my experience might be meaningful to this gathering. By that point, I'd given a few speeches and usually read them as I spoke. This was one of the first times I'd done it off the cuff. Going in, I was very apprehensive. I'd had the same feeling addressing this audience as when we went to see Marlon's wife. Here I was, a guy who'd died and come back. So, why should I survive? Why me instead of their son or daughter or spouse? I was worried that my story might actually have a negative effect. In many respects, I felt ashamed being in front of them, and very vulnerable. I didn't feel like I deserved to be there.

Colonel Kevin Brown, another significant mentor of mine at that time, had grown to be a very close friend because of our heavy interaction at Fort Riley. But more importantly, he was a person who had a naturally deep perspective on the post-trauma experience. He was one of the few I could connect with on this complex topic. Kevin noticed my reservation prior to going on stage. He pulled me aside, placed his hand on my shoulder, and offered some reassuring words that gave me the strength to deliver the talk.

I could only think of two things they might find useful: First, that my last thoughts were of my family and how, when that moment arrives, you really know what's important in your life—family. Your loved ones. Second, to explain what it felt like to die, and that in the very last moment, the very last second, there was such an intense feeling of surrender and peace. There was no pain, no fear. It was a very real, conscious feeling of inner peace and surrender.

After I was done speaking I was nervous and emotional. There are only a handful of times when I've gotten emotional while speaking. I wasn't sure how my words had been received until after the meeting broke for lunch. Right away, there were people lined up to talk with me. They all had questions, many wanted to share their own stories, and some just wanted to thank me. I was relieved.

One who approached me was a mother. Trying so hard to hold back her tears, she said, "My son was much like you. He was athletic, always climbing mountains, lifting weights, and playing sports. He was very active. He was killed by an IED that severed his legs from the waist down. He lived for about thirty minutes before he died. The biggest question I wrestle with every night is if he lost the will to live because he knew he wouldn't be able to walk again. Did he think he wouldn't be accepted by me or by anyone else?"

As she was telling me the story, I got emotional too. But I could absolutely relate to her son. I told her that prior to my injury, I truly believed that I would rather die than lose a limb in combat or live with a major disability. But when I was on the operating table and there was the real possibility that I might have to have my leg amputated, I couldn't have said to the surgeon fast enough, "Take my leg, I'll figure the rest out later." When it was real, staring me in the face, I knew what was really important. The choice between life and a leg was 100 percent clear. Life was the only choice. I said, "If your son was anything like me, he wouldn't let losing his legs get in the way of that. If it were in his power, he would never have given up."

As I was sharing this with her, I could sense the weight coming off her shoulders. Her face relaxed and she smiled, maybe for the first time in a long time. It was powerful. I've had a lot of one-on-ones where the impact on people's lives was clearly felt. But that day really stuck with me.

A CLEAR PRIORITY

General Petersen was at his best when he was driving meetings behind closed doors and developing the staff in small groups or one-on-one. He was strong and focused, but he didn't care much for public speaking events. A Nebraska farm boy at heart, he just didn't care for big crowds. He preferred to get it done, and he did. We spent countless hours together at Fort Riley to support his commanders and staff. He had an impeccable reputation and was the type of person who could bring out the very best in people. Even today, many of his former commanders continue to get promoted through the ranks, which is a powerful indication of his positive influence on the team. Great leaders build great leaders. This is their legacy, and he left a great one behind at Fort Riley. He empowered them to succeed, just as he did me, and remains one of the most meaningful mentors in my life to this day.

But of all the crushing responsibilities that come with being a general, there was one that outweighed them all: helping service members and their families heal from the emotional impacts of combat. Suicide rates were spiking, families were being torn apart, and service members were struggling with inexplicable levels of depression and anxiety as they struggled to resolve the post-trauma experience. This was a DoD-wide problem, not specific to the soldiers of Fort Riley, and we refused to back down until we could find a sustainable solution.

Petersen, Brown, myself, other commanders, and the rest of the staff members worked tirelessly around the clock to impact this situation. It seemed, on a daily basis, we'd receive devastating reminders that we weren't doing enough—every time there was a military funeral, a general officer was present. General Petersen and I went to many,

many funerals. Every week, we'd listen to more accounts of struggling service members, more terrifying stories from their families, and learn of more suicides across the military. The reminder was ever-present, and it took an enormous emotional toll on all of us. We had many late-night conversations about different approaches we could take, exhausting every option we had.

This is, in part, was how I came to enter the speaking circuit. The volume of speaking requests General Petersen received was overwhelming, and we thought we might have an opportunity to impact the paradigm of the discussion surrounding trauma if we utilized my experience to do so. We thought this might be a good opportunity to provide hope to those who were struggling, in addition to educating the community about the true impacts of combat and how we could work together to address the larger problem. We needed all the assistance that we could get.

We already noticed the positive impact that the speaking engagements were having with other organizations, such as Bonnie Carrol's TAPS program and the engagement at West Point, and collectively decided we should continue to push this as hard as we could. If it could help even one person think about trauma differently, it was worth it. This became my top priority.

This was also a very selfless act by General Peterson. An aide-de-camp is an essential role that enhances a general's level of efficiency amidst endless requirements. While I'd still serve as his full-time aide, the speaking engagements would naturally pull me away from some of the more rudimentary responsibilities that came with it. He took much of those things on by himself. We were pulling out all of the stops and taking an unconventional approach, but this sacrifice was necessary in order to serve our soldiers in the best way we could. It was combat, but this time on an invisible and psychological battlefield filled with emotional strife.

THE STIGMA DILEMMA

Leading by example and being willing to take risks with your team is a crucial aspect of building trust. It's a principle shared by virtually every great leader throughout history. Most of us tend to think of this in the context of displaying bravery and courage on the battlefield, but the situation we were facing at Fort Riley required a different type of courage. The courage to be vulnerable.

We were facing a massive challenge overcoming the stigma associated with the behavioral health field. The impacts of emotional trauma were not well understood, and many were hesitant to seek help—they didn't want to risk being labeled as broken, weak, or mentally ill. Moreover, many were concerned that a behavioral health diagnosis would compromise their military career. This posed a major barrier to care. Even if we had the best resources in the world at our disposal, we still needed to get people through the door. It seemed as though those experiencing the most emotional turmoil were also the ones who struggled the most with making the choice to get help.

This isn't just a military problem. It spans across our entire society. The National Institute of Mental Health estimates that only about half of the people who are struggling with a mental health condition seek treatment for it. Anecdotally, we believed that this percentage was even higher in the military.

The Department of Defense began taking aggressive action to overcome this stigma, an effort driven from the top down by the Secretary of Defense himself. Policies were changed, administrative barriers to treatment were removed, and commanders were educated across the armed forces. Programs were also launched that encouraged military personnel, particularly those in leadership roles, to share their personal experiences about seeking treatment. Their willingness to be vulnerable on camera opened the door for many other service members to seek treatment as well. When the commander can demonstrate why something is important, service members tend to follow, be it in combat or in a clinical office. Vulnerability became our most powerful weapon.

Initially, my primary goal in speaking was to reduce or eliminate stigma associated with help-seeking behaviors. But as time went on, I began to realize that there were many more factors surrounding "stigma" than simply being labeled as weak or compromising a career path. While these are valid concerns still present in some organizations, I believe they are often outweighed by much deeper reasons.

Resistance to seeking treatment is significantly more complicated than the fear of being branded as weak; and, in my experience, the most prominent reasons for people not seeking help seem to be internal. Some, particularly those struggling with shame and guilt, don't seek help because they don't think they deserve it. Some have lived in pain for so long that they subconsciously fear what will happen in the absence of it. Others don't seek support because they don't think they'll be believed or understood. Many struggle to understand the weight of what they are experiencing, failing to recognize the importance of getting help and thinking, *How can I talk to a friend or therapist if I can't even describe the feeling that is troubling me?* Yet others don't seek treatment because they don't even realize they could benefit from it.

Perhaps worse is the threat of being labeled with a diagnosis like post-traumatic stress disorder which, unfortunately, so many people are. Frankly, there is a lot of ongoing controversy about what PTSD actually is and what really constitutes a "disorder." Prematurely labeling someone with a disorder can be very damaging. It can reinforce the negative self-beliefs that they're flawed or broken, compounding the sense of hopelessness instead of helping them understand that their responses to traumatic experiences are actually an indication that these functions are *normal* survival instincts. Trauma can leave us frozen in an abnormal state of arousal or stress; but, we absolutely have the power to return to a baseline of normalcy, and even grow stronger with the right approaches.

All of these assumptions and fears had to be overcome—and the resources had to be in place to deliver.

STRATEGIC IMPACT

It didn't take long before the speaking circuit went national. Local interviews turned into top-tier media outlets. Meetings with city leadership turned into meetings with governors, senators, and senior military officials. The message was giving people hope, and the more robust the audience, the more ability we had to turn the "slow-moving ship" in the right direction. Strategically, the talks were also generating a lot of offers of support from leaders in the private and nonprofit sectors. We had a long way to go, but every time something like this occurred, it gave us the sense that something tangible was happening. It drove me to do more.

Today, almost ten years later, I speak professionally around the world. With a very small window of access, usually less than twenty minutes, I'm being pulled in by organizations to transform an entire audience. This is anything but easy. To truly deliver every single time and transform the way people think and feel requires an enormous amount of preparation and practice. For every minute I speak on stage, there are at least ten hours of preparation that goes into it. Speaking at this level is really more of a performance. I'm scrutinizing the use of every single word, how it is inflected, and precisely when it is used. I'm timing my movements on stage to specific aspects of the talk. I'm paying attention to the pace of my voice. I use neurological techniques to recall key transition points, and even visualizing energy systems within the body to project intellect, emotion, or power to match certain components of the talk. All of this is done to enhance the delivery and enrich the experience for the audience.

Back when I first began speaking, I didn't have that level of expertise. But my near-death experience provided a powerful emotional hook that engaged the audience quickly. Any professional speaker will tell you that emotionally engaging an audience is the most important aspect of a talk. Once people are drawn in, it's much more likely that they will be able to internalize and retain the important points of the message.

Essentially, the near-death experience gave us a great platform to work from. I never wanted to share this story just for the sake of sharing a story. I wanted to leverage it for a greater purpose. My thought process on writing this book is no different.

Giving an effective talk can greatly multiply the dissemination of your message. If I speak with someone

one-on-one for twenty minutes and can get that person to internalize the message, it will impact that one person's life. But if I speak to an audience of one thousand people for that same twenty-minute span and I'm able to get all of them to internalize it, I've just multiplied the impact of my message one thousand times over. This is why I take speaking events so seriously. When the message being delivered has the capacity to help people heal, it's importance is elevated even more.

When this all began we faced a behavioral health crisis, and it continues today. Every talk counts—and I put a lot of pressure on myself to deliver.

I wasn't prepared, however, to understand the emotional toll these talks would start to take on me. The message I had was deeply personal, and it required me to revisit and relive those traumatic experiences every single time I went on stage. Although I didn't realize it, I hadn't really processed the deeper aspects of those wounds. I was inadvertently putting myself through a distorted form of prolonged exposure therapy, all while in full view of the public's eye. But with the deep-seeded feelings of survivor's guilt still covertly driving me, I kept going, even if it meant driving myself into the ground to accomplish it. I couldn't just stand by as the crisis was happening, especially when I had a platform to do something about it. At the time, I really didn't feel like my second life was mine to live.

Today, I'm in a very different place. I've processed those

experiences extensively and have relinquished many of the underlying and damaging emotions of the past. As I've continued to heal over the years, the effectiveness of my work has also progressively increased. Back then, I was walking toward the edge of a cliff without knowing it. Because I was still subconsciously suppressing emotion, these deepening challenges remained hidden from the outside world.

PACING

Several months into this effort, I attended a lecture by Kevin Brown at Fort Riley. It was a quarterly awards ceremony designed to recognize community leaders who were making a substantial impact in their respective fields. Kevin has always been a highly engaging speaker with an enviable ability to connect with the audience. His presence drew an audience that packed the room with a couple hundred people.

I stood, as I often did, in the back of the room for events like this to help coordinate any last-minute administrative requirements as an aide-de-camp. If urgent messages came through that needed to get to the leadership team, people could filter them through me, allowing me to approach them at the right time.

Kevin delivered an excellent talk over the next thirty minutes; but, as the audience began to dissipate, he started to walk back toward me. This wasn't uncommon behavior for him. We had a close connection and almost always spoke one-on-one after events. But this time, he looked concerned.

He pulled me aside in a nearby corner, away from the crowd, and said, "Josh, are you doing okay?"

I said, "Yes, sir. Of course."

He said, "Josh, you're pacing."

"Pacing?"

"You've been pacing back and forth the entire time I was on stage, and your mind looks like its somewhere else."

"Sir, I had no idea. I'm okay, though."

Kevin wasn't buying it. He said, "Josh, I know you're taking on a lot, and I know how much pressure you're putting on yourself. What you're disclosing in all of these talks, I know it's not easy. I want you to promise me that you'll call me if you find yourself needing to talk. Don't underestimate this stuff. Know that I'm here for you, and know that I get it. Let's catch up soon."

"Yes, sir." I nodded. "Thank you. I promise you I will."

I really didn't know what to say at the time, or how to respond, but Kevin's words connected with something deep inside me that I couldn't fully understand. Despite being consumed with a major speaking engagement, he still had the presence of mind to notice from the front stage that something was off with me in the back of the room. He did what he needed to do after the event, talking with people and shaking hands, but it was clear that his priority was to get back to me as soon as he could.

Even though I wasn't aware of the emotional state I was in at the time, Kevin's concern, coupled with the immense respect I had for him, made me think twice. It made me take a step back in the moment and realize that I might be walking toward the edge of an emotional cliff without knowing it. Regardless of whether or not it was true, I felt a sense of relief and reassurance knowing that he was there.

In a post-trauma state, we can become so consumed within our own thoughts that they begin to take control of our lives without us realizing it. Sometimes other people in our lives will know more about us than we do. I wasn't aware of the state I was in that day, but having the humility to listen to Kevin's words rather than blow him off was one of the decisions that kept me alive during this journey. It's a two-way street. Kevin had the courage to approach—I had the courage to listen.

In retrospect, perhaps the most important observation to make about this situation is that, all these years later, I don't remember what was circling through my mind that day, but I do clearly remember the words of Kevin Brown.

Chapter 9

The Therapist

BY THE END OF THE FIRST YEAR, I HAD ALREADY DONE over one hundred speaking engagements and interviews. I was held in high regard by those I interacted with, and was looked up to as a "testament to resilience" by the larger public. I was speaking at some of the biggest behavioral health conferences in the world, and was regularly interacting with some of the best clinicians in the country. CNN, FOX News, BBC, and many other media outlets did features on me. I developed a near-clinical understanding of the topic, and received constant accolades from audience members that the message was changing their lives.

Despite all this, I still failed to recognize the symptoms within myself.

After an event in Washington, DC, I found myself standing in the corner of a hotel room, not having a clue who I was anymore. The stress, the pressure, and the crippling sense of guilt could no longer be held at bay. Nothing made sense, and the dull, emotionless void I was experiencing erupted. I drank myself into the ground that night and wanted nothing more than to destroy the false image of myself that I had created. I hated it. I lost all hope, and with very little warning, fell into a deep suicidal spiral fueled by guilt and shame—emotions that finally stepped out of the shadows for the very first time.

Shame is the master emotion, and guilt is its deadly cousin. They are the root cause of chronic traumatic distress and their presence dominates the landscape of the most complex forms of trauma. They also like to remain hidden, controlling your life from the shadows, progressively infecting your soul as if it were a form of cancer.

At that time, in 2009, the broader *national* dialogue surrounding post-traumatic stress rarely included any type of discussion surrounding these covert emotions. Nor were the moral, ethical, and spiritual implications associated with traumatic experiences ever discussed. I don't recall those words being used even once as I was traveling around the country on the speaking circuit, and they never came up during the individual conversations I had with people either (clinician or otherwise).

Most of my focus was on reducing stigma, and most of the vernacular surrounding trauma in a clinical context revolved around the much more recognizable symptoms of arousal and reactive behaviors sometimes experienced in the post-traumatic state. These included things like irritability, aggression, hypervigilance, difficulty concentrating, difficulty sleeping, nightmares, or risk-taking behaviors. I had none of those symptoms.

I went to countless suicide prevention meetings where symptoms like these would be used to teach people about the warning signs of post-traumatic stress, often listed in bullet format on PowerPoint slides. People were told to look out for these signs and encourage others to seek help if they were experiencing them. While these efforts were noble, they weren't hitting home. The suicide rates continued. Anxiety continued. Depression continued. It felt like an endless battle. For some reason, we were missing the mark on what was really behind all of this.

Back then, these arousal symptoms came to define my knowledge of post-traumatic stress, and I knew them cold—but I also wasn't experiencing any of them. With the exception of the short round of nightmares I had while I was withdrawing from methadone during recovery, I never experienced any of these "overt" symptoms of trauma. This led to a dangerous false sense of security. I thought that since I wasn't experiencing any of the "classic" symptoms of post-traumatic stress, the unexplainable deeper void that I *was* facing must just be attributed to exhaustion. In the culture of the military especially, being tired wasn't a reason to stop. I thought I was good. I thought it would eventually ease up.

I was wrong. It wasn't until the moment of this suicidal

collapse that I would start to appreciate the truth behind trauma. Survivor's guilt was causing me to run myself into the ground. I was *unconsciously* trying to run away from the deadly grip it had over my life. The more I ran from the guilt, the further away from myself I became. By then, I felt like a fraud every time I went on stage—totally disconnected and exhausted. Shame was quick to exploit that weakness. I hated myself, and I couldn't explain why.

Some reading this book have experienced moments like this. In a truly suicidal state, the emotional spiral travels so deep that we start to create detailed plans and envision the process. It gains a heavy grip over the psyche and seems to leave no way out.

I found only one thing powerful enough to interrupt the process for me that day: human connection. It had a grounding effect that brought back a fleeting moment of humanness. I was fortunate to recall the commitments I made to people like Kevin Brown, and a select few other people who had the foresight to see this developing. Although I didn't think it would do any good, I placed blind trust and faith into their words and made the decision to reach out to a close friend of mine, Jeff Hall, instead of doing the irreversible. It was a final act of desperation.

HIDING BEHIND THE SHIELD

"If you feel lost, especially if you feel suicidal, reach out to someone. Pick up the phone and call a friend. Make that connection."

That was one of the critical themes I'd focused on in all of my talks over the years leading up to that night. But this was the first time I had to follow my own advice. Up until that moment, I wasn't aware that, with every step I took, I was being controlled by the guilt of surviving and the shame of living. I wasn't aware that I hated myself. I wasn't aware that I was hiding behind the shield of my own story. It was a story so powerful that it concealed the real me—the one who needed help.

My shield came in the form of the message I delivered on stage. Then, several years later when the shame and guilt I thought I had resolved crept back into my life, alcohol abuse and unhealthy relationships served as my shield. All of these behaviors acted in the same manner. They distracted me from facing the truth. While they seemed to help in the moment, they only created more self-destruction in the end. Shame creates a vicious cycle that fuels itself by creating more shame. I wasn't able to break that cycle until I learned to look inward and accept myself first. That is the absolute, rock-bottom truth. While doing this is a journey that ebbs and flows with life itself, that night in the hotel room was the very first step in my process.

As I was picking up the phone, I felt like I was shaking off a dream. I took a few minutes to collect myself and then called Jeff. Like me, he was on the speaking circuit.

We shared the stage several times together. He had also been through extreme combat situations and had lived through the complex emotional turmoil that ensued. He'd done the extensive self-work that allowed him to start the recovery process. Yet I truly believed there was no possible way that even he could understand the rock-bottom point I had reached. His phone went to voicemail and I left him a frightening message. I could barely speak. I was shaking and crying. I felt completely broken.

When I couldn't get Jeff right away, I called Traci Scott who was traveling with us and in DC at the time. Even at that early hour, she picked up. She could hear how distraught I was and came straight to my room. She could see I was in crisis, so she just listened and helped calm me down with her naturally nurturing demeanor. Traci knew what she was dealing with; she'd been a war correspondent for several years and she'd seen and experienced plenty of trauma firsthand. She leveraged her own experiences to empathize with me, giving me the priceless gift of not feeling alone and reminding me of what it felt like to feel human, even momentarily.

A few minutes later, Jeff called back. He listened to me for a bit and then he said something I couldn't believe. It was the one thing I never would have expected him to say. He said, "Good, Josh. I'm so happy for you."

What? How could he say that? I was furious! I wanted to reach through the phone and choke him. I was probably sputtering, saying, "What the hell do you mean?"

Jeff said, "Here's the deal, Josh. I've been working with you for a long time now. I've heard you speak. I've been hearing some of the smaller things you say and the way that you say them. I knew this was going to happen at some point, and I knew that I couldn't talk with you about it until you hit this point on your own. I know you're in pain, but you're actually in a good place, because now it's time for you to begin healing and recovering."

Jeff was a fantastic military tactician, a field artillery officer. He had a tactical level of expertise that few ever attain. Jeff was also brilliant when speaking to soldiers in emotional crisis. He would often "militarize" his vocabulary and use analogies to explain behavioral health concepts in ways they could easily relate to and understand. I wasn't surprised when he continued, telling me, "You have to understand your enemy before you can defeat him. Right now, you're staring your enemy in the eye for the first time."

That was the perfect thing for him to say—it gave me hope, something that only minutes ago seemed gone forever.

TWO FRIENDS

That night, when everything finally erupted, there were many people I could have called, but I called Jeff because I knew his story and I knew he had this depth about him. We were also peers. We were separated by only one rank and had built a strong personal connection over the year.

He had walked down that dark path thinking there was no way to return, and he found his way out. I think I intuitively knew he was the person who could help, even though I truly believed nobody could fully understand. He could and he did. I felt like there was no way to put what I was feeling into words—but with Jeff I didn't have to. Talking to him was like flicking off an emotional switch. All the hot triggers just suddenly went away. I was still struggling, but I was no longer at the most dangerous part of the crisis point. He made me feel like I wasn't alone. Traci's presence, her decision to be there for me was critically important too. I reached out to these two people and they brought me back from a very dark place.

There was more to it than just me reaching out. Like Kevin Brown, Jeff had seen this coming for a long time, and, unbeknownst to me, had actively and consciously set the conditions for me to call him when I reached this point. I clearly remember several occasions when he'd passively checked in with me, drawing my attention to certain statements I'd made or mannerisms I'd displayed that had thrown up red flags. He was progressively testing the waters with me the entire time, and that's what gave me the confidence to call him when it really mattered. Everything he'd said to me suddenly had meaning, and I wanted to know more.

Once I felt a little distance from the crisis point, I knew it was going to be a long road. Jeff doesn't mince words. He said, "It's going to suck. But every difficult step is a step in the right direction." Jeff was my bridge to that path. I was committed to taking his advice and I trusted him, so I knew I could trust the trauma therapist he recommended. Her name was Victoria Bruner. "She goes by Vic. She's really good. She saved my life." I knew he wasn't exaggerating.

Shortly after we hung up, my phone rang. I saw this DC number on the display and I knew it was her. I was nervous to answer. This was a moment of ultimate vulnerability. As soon as she started speaking, her loving and welcoming voice put me at ease. It immediately drew me in. We didn't talk very long. She wanted to see me right away—the next day—so we set up the appointment. Before we ended the call, she said, "Josh, I just want to be sure. Are you okay right now? Do you feel confident you're going to be able to make it to my office?" I knew what she was saying. She was asking if I was in danger of hurting myself or doing something rash. I already knew that she was my lifeline. There was no way I was going to miss that meeting.

A MOMENT OF VULNERABILITY

The next morning I found the general first thing. I'd intended to explain to him as casually and simply as I could what had happened the night before, but I didn't get far into it before totally breaking down in front of him. I started weeping; and I wasn't surprised. He was more like a father figure to me than a general or a boss. Still, it felt embarrassing. I said, "I don't know what's wrong with me." He put his hand on my shoulder, and said, "It's okay, Josh. You're going to be okay and I'm glad you came to me." I told him about the appointment with the therapist. I said, "Sir, I think I should go to this." He agreed, absolutely. Like any great leader, he always had my well-being at the forefront of his mind. Long before this happened, he'd often have talks with me about slowing down the pace. I'd always put on the appearance that I was doing fine, and had unknowingly convinced myself of it.

A couple of hours later I was at Walter Reed, walking down the same path I'd walked when I was recuperating from my sniper wound and still on crutches or in a wheel chair. It felt a little surreal in a way. At the end of a long walk, Vic met me at the door of the building where she had her office. Her whole demeanor was very caring and I immediately felt at ease and even protected by her.

The first time anyone goes through the doors of clinician's office, it's truly an enormous moment of vulnerability. You're putting everything on the line. You're coming to someone as emotionally fragile as you can possibly be. If that vulnerability isn't respected and the experience is bad, it could potentially do more harm than good. It takes a great deal of personal courage to seek help.

That is the essence of what behavioral health clinicians are trusted with. Even though hard science continues to gain traction in the field, there are still substantial elements of clinical work that are more of an art form. Many develop such a high degree of empathy that they can essentially "feel" the state of the person they're working with. It's as if they're stepping out of their own life for a moment and walking with you through yours, all while bringing the added edge of wisdom and perspective to the table. It's an enormously selfless profession. People in these positions are the heroes of an invisible battlefield that's present all over the world. As I was to find, Vic was in the first rank of these specialized clinicians. The best of the best.

As we walked into her office, she turned on this little white noise machine she had by the door. The noise masked voices so that anybody passing by in the corridor wouldn't hear. It's designed to create a private atmosphere so patients can speak freely about their most intimate thoughts and fears. I thought it was kind of funny, actually. I'd been all over national television, spilling my soul on TV, in speeches, and in talks. I felt so exposed that I really could've cared less if some passerby could hear what I had to say. All I wanted to do was make sense of what I was feeling.

As fragile as I was, I felt hope walking into her office. Right before we began the conversation, I looked down and to the left, staring at the floor and briefly reflecting on the last several years. I'd fought through an incurable disease and come back from the dead. I'd graduated from one of the best schools in the world and led men in combat. I'd been selected for one of the most prestigious roles a captain could have, and had already done well over a hundred speaking engagements. It was the first time I'd acknowledged to myself that I'd been through quite a bit in a very short time. I took a deep breath, looked at Vic, smiled, and said, "I'm about to throw a lot at you." Vic didn't flinch. She simply said, "I would love for you to do that." We began.

CLARITY

Vic had basically cleared her appointment calendar for me. To this day, I'm amazed and humbled by that. I spent four hours with her, just me talking the majority of the time. It's all such a blur now that I honestly don't remember many specifics, but I do know that the conversation revolved around me feeling emotionally dead. I had been numb for a long time and had a difficult time feeling any type of emotion whatsoever. I'd never stopped working, pushing myself to the point of burnout because my mind wouldn't allow me to stop. Never could I just sit somewhere comfortably and relax. I didn't even know what that word meant anymore. Happiness and joy were absent from my life and nothing seemed to bring them back. Working out, flying, going hiking. These were things I used to enjoy, but now they had almost no effect. It was also starting to have a noticeable impact on my relationships. Everything I did was mission-based and I had started to hate myself for that. I was living completely inside of my mind.

I was also beginning to question the meaning of my

second life. I could see that my experience had the capacity to help a lot of people, and I had carried that as an inherent responsibility—but I was so disconnected from who I was that I felt like a fraud. I was also so exhausted and depleted that I started to believe my experience was a burden, not a blessing. Perhaps I was brought back to be a slave to that "higher system" or "higher power" I'd so peacefully succumbed to minutes after I was injured. Perhaps I was brought back to create change in our world, and that my own happiness didn't matter. I actually started to accept this thought process. After all, this was just bonus time for me, anyway. I shouldn't be alive.

In moments of frustration, I would say, "I just don't know what's wrong with me." I said that at least a half-dozen times. Vic was a patient listener, but whenever I said that she would always jump in, and say, "There is nothing wrong with you, Josh." She found a few powerful ways to help me understand that.

During the TEDx talk I delivered in 2015, I said that "giving someone the feeling that they're not alone anymore is one of the most selfless gifts you can give to another human being in our lifetime."

That day, Vic gave me that gift. She *normalized* my experience—something I thought was impossible. One by one, she unraveled the complexities of trauma in ways I'd never been exposed to before.

She first focused on my state of emotional withdrawal.

She said, "In combat, you were operating in one of the most chaotic environments imaginable, filled with trauma everywhere. But you were not only operating in it, you were thriving in it. In that environment, you had to learn how to suppress emotion in order to succeed in these incredibly demanding situations. When you do that continuously, when you suppress that emotion, it can fade and shut off completely. When you return to an environment where you're not exposed to trauma, it can be very difficult to turn that emotional switch back on when you've intentionally trained yourself to suppress it for so long."

This made sense. I started recalling many of my experiences in Baghdad, and how often I suppressed my feelings in order to function. This didn't refer only to suppressing fear. I had no room for happiness or sadness to interfere with the mission. I remember hating having to make calls home to talk to my family. It wasn't that I didn't love them, but I hated the feeling of exposing myself to emotional fluctuation. Same with the memorial services we conducted after our comrades were killed. I hated those; I remember not even wanting to go. It felt like a burden, and I didn't want to risk evoking feelings of loss or sadness. I didn't have room for that. I didn't have the energy to go there. It was easier to remain in the cold, focused state I was in. *If I get through this deployment,* I thought, *I'll focus on my family later. I'll honor our fallen later. I'll be able to turn these emotions back on later.* Unfortunately, it's not that easy.

When people struggle with emotional withdrawal, it can cause a painful, shame-based void that conceals our ability to feel human, just as it did for me. This drove the level of self-hatred I was experiencing, and I would've done almost anything to turn it back on. The easiest way to do that is through addictions. Many of us turn to drugs, alcohol, sex, crime, spending excessive amounts of money, and overachieving at work—these things temporarily allow us to *feel* something. To feel alive again. The problem is that these paths can be unhealthy and don't resolve the core issue. Addictions fuel themselves through shame, and the cycle is perpetual unless the root cause is uncovered and addressed.

That root cause of emotional turmoil is often grounded in moral and ethical wounds. Traumatic experiences are traumatic because they fundamentally alter the way we believe the world *should* work, often sparking deep-seated feelings of shame, powerlessness, betrayal, and guilt. When Vic first exposed me to this concept, things got very, very real. It was the first thing that felt right to me in a long time. The demons surrounding me were hiding in places I didn't even know to look. It wasn't about the "big trauma" of getting shot. It wasn't even about death. It was about everything else that surrounded those things.

Our four-hour conversation went by fast. But within that time, she was able to help me uncover and release some of the greatest burdens I was carrying, normalizing the experience along the way. Most importantly, Vic helped me acquire the most valuable tool I needed to move forward with the healing process. *Perspective.*

Shame likes to hide in the shadows. But it does have a weakness, and that weakness can be exploited by shining light upon it and identifying it. Exposing those demons and placing them back into context was the catalyst that sparked the beginning of a lifelong healing process for me. Once I knew what I was facing, once I had a grip on the truth behind trauma, it was impossible to turn back.

A NEW GUILT

Toward the end of our session, Vic said, "Josh, I highly recommend that you back off of the speaking for a while and give yourself the chance to work through some of this for yourself." I saw the wisdom in that, but I walked out of her office feeling even more determined to go out and modify the things I'd been speaking about in order to provide this vitally important information to the thousands and thousands of people who needed it. At the same time, I felt an immediate sense of responsibility. Here I'd been on the national speaking circuit, encouraging people to go seek this help, but I failed to understand it enough myself to resonate with the people who actually needed it the most. Vic's information was cutting edge and not yet mainstream, but I intuitively knew that it was quite possibly the key to resolving these challenges at scale. And I had a platform to do something about it.

Rarely does anyone get four hours of a first rate clinician's time when they find themselves at a point of crisis. I was able to meet with Vic because of a connection through a friend. I thought I might've been given more attention because I was an aide-de-camp and because I had some small amount of celebrity status. I was utterly grateful for my access to Vic's generosity in putting her remarkable therapeutic gift to work for me. Yet I couldn't shake the guilt that so many others didn't have access to this level of care.

After my meeting with Vic, I didn't subscribe to continuous therapy, despite her very strong recommendation that I do so. I did recognize that the recovery process was only just beginning and had to find a way to continue to do the self-work needed to heal, while also being able to project this message to a larger audience. I made a commitment to Vic that I'd remain in close contact with her, and would also build out a deliberate support network of clinicians and expert companions closer to Fort Riley, which I did.

Additionally, I was deeply committed to understanding this information in depth and knew there was a long way to go. I'm a highly introspective person and knew that as my knowledge base grew, my ability to understand and heal myself would also grow. I knew it wasn't the ideal image of the therapeutic process, and many people need more consistent professional support, but I trusted my intuition and knew when to leverage support if I needed it. My sense of urgency surrounding the scope of the larger problem really pulled at me, but I was also committed to doing the self-work necessary to continue the healing process, while also helping as many other people as possible join me along the way. The two were mutually supportive, and I knew I needed to stay in the trenches.

Chapter 10

The Leader

I WAS IN A FAIRLY GOOD PLACE IN THE MONTHS AFTER my breakthrough and first meeting with Vic, both emotionally and physically. The pressure hadn't let up, the stress was still relentless, but I had it under control for the most part.

As my time as General Petersen's aide neared its end, several colonels and brigade commanders approached me about taking over command of one of their companies. All of the offers were humbling. A brigade commander is a prestigious and powerful position with a huge scope of responsibility. I didn't want to turn down any of them, so I asked General Peterson for advice to get his take on where I could have the biggest impact. I was fully expecting to take command of one of the infantry companies for a deployment to Afghanistan or Iraq. To command a company in combat is the pinnacle assignment of a captain's career. The responsibility is enormous and I felt it's where I belonged.

But the commander at Fort Riley's hospital and General

Peterson had another idea for me. They asked me if I would be willing to take a company command in the Warrior Transition Unit. The WTU supports soldiers with physical and emotional injuries who require extensive, specialized care. Now that I had some background in the behavioral health field, they felt I was a natural for this assignment, and my experience sustaining a severe injury in combat would help me better relate to the soldiers in that population. I also lived with the debilitating effects of Crohn's disease, and had a great deal of empathy for those who struggled with incurable, life-long illnesses.

Selecting me to command a WTU company made sense, but I had some reservations. I knew it was an important role, but I was still focused on getting back downrange to a deployment in the Middle East. It was the same feeling I had years before at West Point. I felt I needed to be part of the main effort, and, at the moment, that effort was in Iraq and Afghanistan.

There was one more daunting detail. The WTU was the highest risk unit in the division. The unit had a high density of soldiers who had complex behavioral health conditions, often coupled with severe physical injuries. Many of them were about to lose their careers due to those injuries. All that added up to daily clashes and crisis de-escalation. The stress can be off the charts. I also knew from my two years working as an aide that the WTU was facing a lot of problems. The challenges were extensive, but I felt confident that I could make an impact, so I told the general I would take over the command.

MAKING THE TRANSITION

The Warrior Transition Unit was created by the Department of Defense to provide focused medical attention to severely wounded service members returning from Iraq and Afghanistan. With advancements in battlefield medical technology, wounded soldiers like myself are surviving injuries that they rarely would have survived before. Many are coming home with severe disfigurements, burns, and amputations that present trials they must learn to overcome. Often, injuries like this bring with them life-long physical pain that must be carefully managed. While more of our soldiers are surviving, the ensuing struggle to regain a sense of inner peace can be crippling, naturally exposing them to significant emotional challenges.

Conditions like these are ever-present; it's difficult to describe the deep emotional toll they can take on someone over time. Even the most resilient person can falter. My injury in Baghdad was acute and I recovered in just a few months, but I'll live with the looming threat of a Crohn's relapse for the rest of my life. At any time, this disease could flare-up for no apparent reason. I could be fine today, but then experience chronic pain and fatigue tomorrow that I'd be fighting through for months to come. I've lived with this disease for over ten years now, and it's been an emotional roller coaster ride ever since. I'd reach highs of being in peak physical condition and full of energy, only to be ripped back down into a trough of rapid weight loss, extreme pain, and chronic fatigue. It's a perpetual cycle of euphoric highs and utterly depressing lows that made me feel like a modern-day Sisyphus. I've often said that I'd go through the experience of getting shot ten times over if I could trade it for living free from Crohn's disease.

Successful treatment of complex medical conditions like these hinges on an integrated treatment approach where all conditions affecting an individual are addressed simultaneously in a comprehensive fashion. Those with complex medical circumstances often have multiple medical appointments per day with providers in various fields. The healing process is time consuming, sometimes requiring you to take a step back from your normal life to exclusively dedicate yourself to that process. The Warrior Transition Unit was established to give our most severely wounded soldiers the opportunity to do just that.

Today, there are Warrior Transition Units at many military bases all across the US; but back then in 2007, the Department of Defense had just established the first of these units at Walter Reed. The purpose of this unit was to either help soldiers return to the military or, in the event that their injuries were too severe for continued military service, help them make a successful transition to civilian life. The soldiers in this unit were able to narrow their mission to one goal: healing. That's it. You're not assigned other tasks. Your exclusive focus is on self-healing and recovery.

After my injury in Iraq, I didn't have much interaction with the WTU. I was already demonstrating positive signs of advanced recovery and my attitude was laser focused on getting back to Baghdad. I was also taking personal initiatives to get myself combat-ready. That's what I wanted. I just needed the freedom and the time to heal and I took advantage of it.

The person I'd been assigned to administratively was a three-time-deployed sergeant first class and fellow infantryman. We made an instant connection. When I told him I was planning to go back to Baghdad as soon as possible, he understood completely and just asked me to continue what I was doing. He didn't need to exert a lot of oversight with me. I would check in with him every day to let him know I was okay, but outside of that I pretty much stayed under the radar and focused on returning to Baghdad. Little did I know that, in just a couple of years, these circumstances would be flipped and I'd be heading up my own Warrior Transition Unit.

THE SOLDIERS

When I took over a company in the WTU at Fort Riley, I knew that the unit was struggling. As an aide-de-camp, I'd been present for briefings that outlined the challenges of the unit. I knew I was walking into a difficult assignment, but when I finally got on the ground, so to speak, and interacted with the people and made a true assessment, I found that the problems were worse than I thought. Despite many of its benefits.

The WTU admits patients based on the complexity of their medical care. The more extensive the treatment plan, the higher the likelihood that the soldier would be assigned to this unit. Initially, admissions into this unit due to injuries or wounds sustained in combat dominated its population. Over the next several years, however, behavioral health challenges became the most prevalent concern. As I mentioned earlier, the chronic persistence of pain derived from injury or disease has devastating emotional effects and can lead to depression. This, coupled with the possibility of a career-ending injury, prompted many to struggle with their central purpose and their meaning in life. The military is an environment grounded in camaraderie and brotherhood, and serving a cause much greater than yourself can be extremely meaningful and perhaps even necessary to lead a fulfilling life. As German philosopher Friedrich Nietzsche stated, "He who has a *why* to live for can bear almost any *how*."[2] After sacrificing so much, many of the men and women in this unit were suddenly faced with the possibility of letting it all go as they struggled to redefine their purpose in life.

This was also the first time many of these soldiers had

---

2   Viktor Frankl, *Man's Search for Meaning* (Beacon Press: Boston, 2006), 76.

slowed down. Most of them had been running at a hundred miles per hour, deployment after deployment, training after training, but now they were forced to a halt in the face of their injuries. The rapid pace soldiers maintain tends to serve as an inadvertent emotional shield, allowing them to suppress their emotions and "deal with it later." But when that pace is taken away and they're forced to slow down, the emotions that they try to bury have an opportunity to resurface. All these conditions contributed to making the WTU an ultra-high-risk organization.

I remembered how this felt from my time as a soldier in recovery at the Water Reed WTU. It was tough to be surrounded by people with so many injuries. I actually felt *guilty* about my ability to heal. I was one of the very few who was expected to make a full recovery. Yet, all around me, I was constantly reminded of those not so fortunate. The image of a beautiful young girl in her early twenties pushing her young, double-amputee fiancé around in a wheelchair is one that I'll never forget. They'd have to learn how to re-dream their dreams and make new ones—their innocence taken away. My guilt was constantly being triggered in one way or another. I felt guilty for being the lucky one who could make a full recovery when so many others couldn't, while simultaneously feeling guilty about not being with my men downrange. I was in a constant state of emotional turmoil.

I was always resistant to labelling this as "survivor's

guilt." I didn't fault myself for Harper's death. Everything we did that day was tactically sound, and I think it actually helped knowing that I nearly died with him. Moreover, we knew that something like this could happen because of the nature of our environment. The term survivor's guilt almost implies that we had to have done something wrong to feel guilty about surviving.

I had a long conversation about this topic with a close friend and mentor of mine, Dr. Bob Koffman, a top military psychiatrist, and I've come to understand that survivor's guilt has a much broader underlying meaning. Although I didn't blame myself for Harper's death, he died and I lived. That's a fact that will not change. It likely contributed to the irrational intensity I carried after deployment to make up for that loss and fill the void.

More importantly, survivor's guilt isn't just about direct involvement with life and death. This was driving the guilt I felt at West Point when my friends and classmates were killed in combat—I felt helpless to do anything about it, trapped in my academic environment. When I was at Walter Reed, the survivor's guilt I experienced was more about my ability to survive and fully heal from a devastating injury when so many others couldn't. It was a guilt surrounding my men still being in combat and being in extreme danger, while I was lying safe in a hospital bed. It was also the guilt of having a platform to influence the paradigm of the behavioral health field, and still seeing so many people lose their lives every single day to suicide. As I concluded my conversation with Bob that night, I realized that survivor's guilt was actually one of the primary factors driving me to the edge. It's a universal phenomenon that impacts us when we experience loss. And it is powerful.

Upon taking command of the WTU years later, I realized that many of the people in that unit struggled with similar challenges, and I soon came to realize this would be the most intense assignment of my military career—even more intense than patrolling the streets of Baghdad.

A TEST OF LEADERSHIP

At Fort Riley, one of the most challenging cases we encountered was a soldier who wouldn't shave or wear his uniform, and refused to attend morning formations. He isolated himself in his room, interacting with people as little as possible. He struggled with multiple medical challenges, including PTSD, depression, and chronic pain.

This was one of the first soldiers brought to my attention upon taking command of the unit. The cadre member responsible for him was frustrated and didn't know what to do. His clinical social worker also approached me and was highly concerned. She had over twenty years of experience in this field and was a fantastic clinician, but she was struggling to make any progress with this individual during session. Both the cadre member and the social worker asked if I would be willing to speak with this soldier one-on-one, in the hopes that I'd be able to resonate with him.

When I met him the next morning, he walked into my office wearing civilian clothes and with a full beard. His attitude was casually disrespectful and he initially seemed disinterested in what I had to say. Fortunately, I was able to build that relationship quickly by talking with him about my experience of getting shot in Baghdad. Then, I introduced him to the concept of the moral and ethical impacts of combat. I told him about my crashing point in the hotel room in Washington, DC—my vulnerability, my complete emotional unraveling, my suicidal moments of deep despair, my darker soul.

That soldier and I talked for about three hours, in a conversation similar to my long session with Vic. When we were done, he shook my hand. I think he was surprised that I didn't order him to wear his uniform. I didn't even bring it up. I didn't bring up the beard either. I wasn't looking at him from a military standpoint, but as a human being who needed to heal. I could see his potential. I knew the beard and the clothing weren't meant as deliberate disrespect. He had deeper reasons he couldn't get out quite yet. Instinctively, I could *feel* something about him and his situation that gave me hope.

After this productive conversation, the last thing I was going to do was order him to shave and wear his uniform. I knew that would be futile and counterproductive. I really didn't care what the military regulations called for. I cared about accomplishing my mission, which was to help him heal.

That man later told me that our conversation made a huge impact on him; it was the first time an officer had actually listened to him. He could tell I genuinely cared, and he appreciated that I didn't try to force military policy on him when it simply wasn't important in our lives at that point. As I would come to find out, there were very clear and profound reasons why he stopped wearing his uniform. He used to be the top-rated soldier in his unit and was considered to be the definition of a great non-commissioned officer. He was the example that everyone else looked up to.

During his deployment, however, he was surrounded by poor leaders who essentially abandoned him and the rest of his team. Officers in his unit refused to go out on patrol and chose to run their operations over the radio while he and his men were in harm's way. This caused an invalidation of his beliefs about the military. Compounding that was his subsequent diagnosis of having a medical condition which required a medication that made him gain excess weight. Physically, he felt like he was so out of shape that he would be disgracing the uniform if he wore it. He was far from the disrespectful soldier many believed he was. Fortunately, my life experiences positioned me to sense the true person he was and support him from that moment forward. He later went on to participate in extensive therapy and made a successful transition out of the military. He also became an advocate and mentor for other soldiers in the unit, which helped him regain his sense of self-worth.

At his discharge a year and a half later, I conducted my change of command ceremony and found him in the front row with a couple of other men who had also refused to wear their uniforms. All of them were standing in formation, all of them in uniform, and all clean shaven, though I had never asked them to. I didn't have to. As successful as the situation with this soldier eventually became, it's complexity is representative of the many levels of challenges we wrestled with on a daily basis.

STABILITY

In addition to individual cases, we had to take a comprehensive approach to stabilizing the unit as a whole. I knew early on that the resources we had at our disposal would not be enough, and that we would have to get creative to make up for those gaps. We pulled out every resource we could muster to add value to the organization. We partnered with the nearby Kansas State University to create art therapy and drama therapy programs for the soldiers. We also tied into local police departments to train our cadre on crisis de-escalation techniques. I trained our therapists on the complexities of counterinsurgency so they could better understand the environment returning soldiers were exposed to. And the list goes on. We continuously sought ways to improve the organization.

Two of those efforts made notable positive impacts. The first was introducing a therapeutic retreat to Fort Riley modeled after the National Veterans Wellness and Healing Center based in Angel Fire, New Mexico. This nonprofit organization provides intensive therapeutic retreats to veterans and their spouses. Over the course of one week, members of the retreat are exposed to traditional therapeutic approaches such as group, couples, and individual therapy, while also gaining exposure to the emerging holistic modalities such as yoga, reiki, massage, equine therapy, dance therapy, and Native American spiritual healing.

The fundamental principles of the retreat are even more compelling. Their insistence on treating the family (or couple) as a whole, instead of just individually, allows couples to approach the healing process together. The retreat also puts a deliberate emphasis on intergenerational interaction, allowing veterans from multiple generations to connect and heal together. When I attended this retreat, we had couples from every combat generation represented, from World War II forward. While the location and time of the conflicts may have been separated by decades, the emotional challenges faced by the couples were nearly identical.

Finally, the community-based nature of the retreat

allows its organizers to leverage resources already available within the community. The end results are powerful. Many of the people who attend this retreat find themselves opening up about their experiences for the very first time. For some, it establishes the foundation of their healing process. For others, it serves as a gateway to further care.

BODY, MIND, AND SPIRIT

A true healing process involves healing the mind, body, and spirit, as trauma impacts each of these components differently. When integrated together in a treatment approach, the results are compelling. Unfortunately, many of the therapeutic approaches used in the behavioral health field focus exclusively on the mind. While cognitive approaches like cognitive behavioral therapy and prolonged exposure therapy are a vital component of healing, they often fall short of facilitating a true transformation when done in isolation.

In today's society, we tend to live inside of our minds. Cognition dominates us and many people inadvertently become disconnected from their bodies. Moreover, many struggle with a limited sense of spirituality as well, a connection to something greater than themselves. An ideal treatment approach will enhance all three.

When I first met with Vic, I was living exclusively inside of my mind. While I was able to resolve many of the mental processes surrounding trauma, I found that it only got me so far. Vic predicted this and extended an invitation to participate in the Angel Fire retreat just prior to taking command of the WTU. As it turned out, it was among the most powerful experiences of my life.

Angel Fire's approach allowed me to begin to get back in touch with my body, while also reconnecting to a sense of spirituality that I had neglected for a long time. I participated in yoga for the first time, was exposed to therapeutic massage, and had a powerful first experience with Reiki (energy work). The beauty of these techniques is that they allow us to release trauma that is literally stored within the body's memory, something that can't be approached cognitively. Moreover, modern science is proving that these techniques not only work, but are a vital necessity for healing and transformation.

The program also incorporated Native American spiritual healing ceremonies that have traditionally been practiced for thousands of years. Of everything I experienced during the retreat, these ceremonies had the most significant impact on me moving forward. They allowed me to regain a sense that we're part of something much greater than ourselves, and I began to accept and revisit the validity of the powerful and peaceful sense of surrender I experienced at the point of death.

IMPORTED ANGEL FIRE

We couldn't mimic the Angel Fire model exactly at Fort

Riley because Angel Fire leveraged assets that were embedded within their specific community. So, when we staged our retreat in Kansas, we utilized assets within our own community to achieve similar effects. The challenge was to build relationships with the various organizations and people who were going to support it, which would ensure it would be equally effective. To bring this effort together and make it work, I called on the generous assistance of Vic Bruner and Dr. Briana Goff of Kansas State University, along with Chuck Howe (the CEO of Angel Fire). Some generous grants from Kansas State University—facilitated by Dr. Goff—also made a big difference in our nonprofit venture. Kansas State University's Institute for the Health and Security of Military Families, led by Dr. Goff, continues to drive cutting-edge research in the field to this day.

In addition to sessions that employed traditional therapies, we also incorporated yoga, Native American spiritual healing, therapeutic artwork, and combat poetry. With the poetry, we were also able to interject an all-important element of intergenerational interaction by inviting my close friend and Vietnam veteran John Musgrave. His book *Notes to the Man Who Shot Me* is considered a classic in the combat poetry genre. John is a truly inspirational person whose perspective on combat trauma is deeper than anyone I know. He was shot point-blank in the chest when his unit was ambushed, and, like me, was also resurrected from the dead.

John and I met in a strange way, back when I was an aide-de-camp on a speaking tour. Jeff Hall was there too, also slated to speak. We were at an American Legion rally in a remote part of Kansas. It was an outdoor event in the middle of a field and it was raining, so the turnout wasn't very good. My turn to speak was coming up, but there was one person on before me, an older guy with a gray beard. He was wearing a camouflage coat, and as he walked up the steps to the stage he looked like a stereotypical image of a Vietnam veteran. I'm utterly ashamed to admit it, but Jeff and I exchanged glances, like, "Oh boy. Here we go with another anti-war speech from a disgruntled veteran." I ended up eating those thoughts in a hurry. From the moment John opened his mouth and began reading his poetry to the moment he concluded, I was riveted. Jeff and I were literally speechless. I've never been so completely captivated by a speaker. When he was done and I took the stage, I felt like I had nothing to say.

John and I became excellent friends after that and I was thrilled that he'd agreed to participate in our first retreat. He lived fairly close to Fort Riley, so he was often involved with my work there. When I called and told him I could use his help, he knew the need was real. He was deeply involved with our activities on the day he attended the retreat. He read some of his poems, of course, and by the time he finished we were all in tears. Even the combat veterans who were hesitant to open up were clearly moved. I've seen this many times. John's poetry is simple and straightforward, but disarmingly powerful at the same time.

John participated in all the therapeutic sessions that day. For the Iraq and Afghanistan veterans, connecting with a person like John can be a life-altering experience. Veterans from John's generation have struggled for decades. They didn't have access to the level of care that we have today. In fact, they were largely disgraced when they came back from the war.

If you go to the Vietnam Memorial in Washington, DC, and look at the 58,286 names engraved on the wall of those killed in combat, just imagine being able to go to the other side of the walkway to read the names of the Vietnam veterans who committed suicide *after* the war. If those names were also memorialized, the Vietnam memorial would be twice its current size.

Those who survived the war *and* the homecoming had to work through their emotional challenges largely on their own. Many naturally gravitated toward one another for support. John turned to poetry to explore his experience and understand the trauma behind it, and his survival is a testament to the deep wells of strength we all have within us to persevere and transform. I only wish I could take every troubled veteran and sit him down for an hour, one-on-one, with John Musgrave. Nobody has a deeper perspective on trauma and combat stress.

WEARY WARRIORS

The Native American healing component of our retreat was especially successful. The healer was also a Korean War veteran, which made it all the more powerful.

On the final night of the retreat, we gathered the participants around a fire and the healer conducted a traditional welcome home ceremony for warriors that was specific to the customs of his tribe. The ceremony began by facing east, in the direction of the rising sun, symbolizing the dawn of a new day for weary warriors. As we stood in a circle around the fire, everyone was silent. It's difficult to describe the type of energy you feel in that setting. There's something almost mystical about it, frozen in time, with the smell of campfire and burning sage ever-present. John Musgrave joined us for that ceremony. When it was finished, we all went back inside and John read his poetry. It was a powerful ending to the retreat.

During the healing ceremony and John's poetry, I had a strong sense of gratification in seeing the positive impact it had on the couples in the room. After that, everyone headed to bed, exhausted and emotionally spent. I'd worked pretty much around the clock leading up to the retreat, but I found I was too tired to sleep. I was a little overwhelmed with emotion and energy, having put enormous personal effort into making it all happen and seeing it come together. My mind was racing. I got out of bed and came back out to the fireplace where the embers of the fire were still burning and the wood smoke aroma filled the night air. It was a beautiful, clear night with a sky full of stars. I felt energized but quite peaceful at the same time. It was a rare moment to finally exhale, let myself relax, and just breathe.

A few minutes after I had settled in, I noticed someone heading toward the fireplace. It was John. He couldn't sleep either so he came out to sit by the last of the fire. We didn't say much. We were both there for the same thing, to catch a little bit of the peace of the night and the nurturing calm that the healing ceremony had left behind. I couldn't help but see us as these two tired warriors from different generations, separated by decades, but both of us still pressing forward, trying to make sense of the burden and the beauty of two darker souls.

The retreat was measurably successful for many of the attending soldiers. At the end of the experience, several participants who were previously resistant to therapy agreed to attend more extensive treatment. They committed to working on their experiences and processing them through intensive therapy in conjunction with their spouses. The retreat experience empowered them to take an active role in their healing process.

BOOSTING OUR BANDWIDTH

As the relationship strengthened with my team of therapists, I was regularly called upon by our clinicians to work with soldiers on a one-on-one basis. My objective wasn't to be their therapist, but rather to serve as a bridge to further therapy. If our clinicians had trouble resonating with a struggling soldier, I'd work with that individual. Typically, after spending some time with me, they'd be far more open and willing to commit to working with their primary therapist.

Over time, you develop a feel for how to quickly go deep with someone, actively listen, and empathize. You have to become emotionally engaged and always alert. If I'm not fully engaged, I might miss a key word or voice inflection that could be critical to opening up another door into their mind. I might miss the hint or inconsistency in the story, or details that are skipped over. Signs like this are often indicators that an individual hasn't fully processed their experience. No matter how exhausted you might be from a long, emotional session, you can't ease up or you might miss the cry for help that's subconsciously coming out through their words or mannerisms. I'm always looking for the opportunity to leverage subtle hints, to dive deeper with the individual when it's appropriate and safe.

After numerous sessions, listening to so many troubled people talk about the greatest vulnerabilities in their lives—in addition to all of my other responsibilities of command—I found it impossible to manage so many cases on an individual basis. The unit was growing and I found I was pushing myself to the point of extreme burnout. I wasn't achieving the larger effect I wanted. I could work with people one-on-one and be successful, but with hundreds of other soldiers in need of the same level of care, I knew we had to find another approach.

We collectively decided to initiate a therapeutic support group that I would personally facilitate. I worked closely with the primary therapists to shape the group dynamics in advance by identifying people with similar experiences and backgrounds. The group would meet twice per week, three hours per session, for a total of eight sessions over the course of a month. Typically, about ten to twelve participants were invited for each iteration.

AGAIN, ACROSS THE DECADES

One of the sessions that consistently emerged as significantly beneficial for the participants was a session that included Vietnam veterans. John Musgrave and I thought it would be valuable to simply put Vietnam and Iraq/Afghanistan veterans together in the same room over dinner and just let them talk (with some subtle guiding from John and I to ensure the discussion was productive).

John and I joined a couple of other really great Vietnam veterans John pulled in from the local community. Of course, John had specifically selected two of his friends he knew had perspectives on trauma that ran as deep as his own. They were articulate fellows who were more than happy to offer their wisdom to a younger generation of combat veterans. Just as I'd seen at Angel Fire, and just as

I'd seen in the Angel Fire-inspired retreat we conducted near Fort Riley, this blending of the generations was a very powerful approach. For the younger veterans, it was tremendously inspiring to meet what you might call their tribal elders—men of age and wisdom who had seen the horrors of war, survived, found ways to cope, and made the best lives for themselves that they could. At the same time, you could tell that the older generation were seeing themselves in the younger soldiers who had been through their own grueling experiences.

Despite the age differences, they were brothers in arms, separated by decades but brought together in that moment, and sharing a profound respect. The Iraq and Afghanistan veterans would be in awe, asking, "How did you manage to operate in the jungles of Vietnam under those extreme conditions with firefight after firefight?" But then the Vietnam veterans would say, "Well I don't know how *you* did it. You had to go through multiple deployments. We were usually one and out." This bedrock of mutual respect was an amazing thing to see. Within about five minutes, you'd have thought they'd all been deployed together in the same unit.

When you're a young veteran and you're in the company of Vietnam veterans who've been living with their trauma for over forty years, a feeling develops that you've finally found someone who understands you, totally and completely. You don't need to say everything—they simply get it. In the larger scheme, that becomes a platform for further discussion of the experience and lends itself to further progress. It enhances the sense of human connection. It dispels the sense of isolation. It allows you to be understood without having to articulate every detail of the complex emotions you probably don't even understand yourself. The Iraq and Afghanistan veterans would say, every single time, "I got more out of that session than I could have ever imagined." And the Vietnam veterans would invariably say the same thing, "I think I got more out of this session than they did."

The Vietnam veterans didn't get much behavioral health support (if any), or any kind of help at all when they returned from war. Many of them just learned to do it on their own. Those who survived *after* the war learned to cope through introspection, they learned through pain, through suppression, and through trial and error. Those who could leaned on each other for support, and still do. Many thousands of them couldn't bear it all and took their own lives. For years, the image of a Vietnam veteran was a stereotype on TV and in the movies. They were portrayed as loons with short fuses, ready to blow, and then they had to figure out on their own how to live with that indignity too. So, for John and the other Vietnam veterans who were there, I know this simple dinner gave them a heightened sense of purpose to connect with this generation of combat veterans who were just a bit younger than their own children. All those years and all that pain, suddenly it was not for nothing. It was valued and respected.

We conducted about eight different iterations of this group process while I was in command, treating roughly one hundred soldiers, most of whom committed to ongoing therapy afterward. It was the pinnacle of achieving an integrated approach. It maximized the impact that our team had on the organization as a whole and garnered support from everyone in the unit. Most importantly, it helped many troubled souls and their spouses begin to regain a sense of inner peace and hope for the future. Without question, my proudest professional accomplishment was creating and leading these groups, and watching the entire unit unlock its true potential.

But I underestimated the enormous personal toll it was taking on me.

Chapter 11

The Truth

THERAPISTS HAVE ONE OF THE MOST EMOTIONALLY demanding jobs in existence. They are walking people through their greatest moments of pain and vulnerability. It is imperative that they remain fully engaged and present with the client during session. If they come to the office feeling "off" in any way, it can limit their ability to pick up on crucial indicators (both verbal and non-verbal) that could otherwise be used as windows or clues into the individual's healing process. They have to be on their game at all times.

This isn't easy, and it's not something that can be taught from a book. It requires a high degree of empathy and a willingness to give their energy to someone else. Most therapists I know are exhausted and emotionally spent by the end of the day, particularly when they have a high case load and are seeing clients back-to-back. This exposes them to the debilitating effects of compassion fatigue and vicarious traumatization.

Compassion fatigue occurs when you give too much of yourself to others. If we offer every ounce of our empathy and energy to our clients, there is nothing left for us to fall back on. Eventually, we end up trying to draw from an empty well of energy.

With vicarious traumatization, people are indirectly traumatized by the experiences of others. This can lead to effects that are similar to the traumatic experience itself. My stepfather's most difficult time throughout his twenty-five-year police career was when he spent three years investigating nothing by sex crimes. Every day, he went detail by detail, question by question, uncovering the most horrific experiences imaginable. With that depth of immersion, you can find yourself living within the experience itself. Therapists, naturally, explore those same situations. They walk with people through their deepest pain to uncover details that can help them better understand it and move forward in the healing process. I equate this to someone being trapped in hell, completely alone, and unable to navigate a way out. Sometimes, we have to walk through hell with them in order to guide them back to safety. Doing this repeatedly can expose anyone to dangerous levels of fatigue.

This is why therapists are trained in school to guard themselves against these things to remain fully present with their clients. Many maintain strict office hours in order to provide adequate time to decompress. Others deliberately build in time in between sessions to meditate, clear their minds, and reset before working with the next client. Some limit the number of highly complex patients they take on in order to avoid being overloaded with extreme back-to-back emotional experiences. Many therapists also go to therapy themselves on a regular basis, just for "maintenance." All of these techniques are applied to guard a person against burnout, which is an easy line to cross in this field.

I never had such training. Even if I had, I doubt I would've applied it effectively at that time. I was competing with the weight and pressure of command. I was responsible for the lives of the soldiers in my unit, and, just as I had throughout my career in every leadership role I assumed, I gave myself fully to my team. I was also committed to not only repairing the unit, but expanding those efforts across the country to add value to the system as a whole. I didn't take much pride in helping a hundred people. I wanted to help a hundred thousand. If we had systems in place that worked, I saw no reason why they shouldn't be expanded to help a broader population. Someone had to make that happen, and I had a platform to help us do it. Because of that, I was driven by a deep sense of responsibility and commitment to others.

Although I wasn't a therapist, I frequently held extensive one-on-one sessions with soldiers, often at the request of their primary therapist. I was also facilitating the support group. My objective was to serve as a bridge to further treatment, but getting to that point often required me to give every ounce of my being to the people I worked with. A high level of trust developed between me and many of the soldiers. Many committed to active therapy (which was excellent), but late at night, when most of the providers were home, the soldiers would reach crisis points and often reach out to me personally.

In one situation, I had a soldier call me around 3:00 a.m. one morning. When I asked him what was going on, he calmly replied, "I'm driving to Wichita." I asked, "Why are you doing that, buddy?" and he said, "My friend who was killed in Iraq is sitting next to me."

This wasn't good. Over the course of the next few minutes, I was able to talk the individual into turning around and coming back to Fort Riley. He agreed to meet me and the medical team at the office. Meanwhile, his mother, who was naturally in a state of panic, was contacting me as well. After he was safely returned and we stabilized his situation, I drove out to his mother's house to talk with her for a while and help her understand what was happening with her son.

Our ability to handle this situation was a success. The soldier displaying the strength to call me, instead of doing something irreversible, was also a major success. It was a testament to his courage and the level of trust we'd established. In moments of crisis, this is *exactly* what we want to see happen. It took a lot of effort and teamwork to foster this type of environment.

All of this might have been manageable if these situations occurred occasionally and we had the time available to emotionally reset, but they occurred quite frequently. Nearly every day, I would work with soldiers on a one-on-one basis and facilitate the support group. At the same time, I was traveling frequently—several times each month—to speaking engagements that were booked all over the country. After a few months, I realized that I couldn't escape it. I felt like I had to stay "on" all of the time. Internally, I was beginning to collapse.

LYING IN WAIT

The first indication that something was wrong came while my then-wife and I were driving to Pennsylvania over Christmas in 2011. We stopped at a hotel in St. Louis for the night and had a light but healthy dinner with her parents. Not an hour later, I was balled up with severe stomach pain and could barely walk back to the car. It was the beginning of a Crohn's disease flare-up.

I'd been through some minor flare-ups before, all of which I was able to overcome, either naturally or with a short round of Prednisone to suppress the symptoms. Outside of that, I attempted to manage the disease without the use of medication. I was convinced that staying physically active and maintaining a great diet could keep the disease at bay. I resisted the idea of medication because it could have compromised my military career.

But that night was different. The extreme pain was caused by a bowel obstruction which I hadn't experienced before. I spent the next eight hours doubled over, curled up into a fetal position on the bathroom floor of our hotel room. I was dry heaving, drenched in sweat, and literally wanted to die. My wife felt helpless and begged me to go to the hospital. After seeing the impact it had on her, I agreed to go to the emergency room in the morning. By that time though, the worst of the symptoms had passed, so we skipped the ER and made our way back to Kansas.

When I had experienced symptoms similar to this before, I usually snapped back within a few days. This time, I didn't get better. I got worse. I got weaker and felt horrible. I would often lock my office door and curl up on my desk to minimize the pain. Sometimes the fatigue was so overwhelming that I'd ask my medic to come to my office and give me IVs of saline, just to keep me going. I couldn't eat and was scared to try. Over the year that followed, I was essentially living off of a six pack of Ensure Plus per day. It was the only thing I could safely consume without triggering symptoms.

To make matters worse, I didn't slow down at work and just tried to push through. Taking extended time off meant that our efforts would be compromised. Compromised, in this case, meant that people were in danger of losing their lives to suicide. To me, this was a very real life-or-death situation, similar to combat, and I couldn't just back off.

It was as real as it could get. There was a relentless sense of urgency behind everything we were doing. On top of it all, another dark factor was now driving me; the feeling that it was "me versus the disease," and I couldn't allow Crohn's to win.

Eventually, the physician I worked with noticed my state and implored me to get help. I hated to do it, but I was beginning to fear I was killing myself. I'd already lost more than thirty pounds, and my weight was continuing to drop. She placed me on forty milligrams of Prednisone per day to help stabilize my condition and also lined me up for an appointment with a gastroenterologist.

I knew how it would go. He'd order a colonoscopy and some other tests. Then he'd prescribe medications. The typical medications for Crohn's are biologic drugs that have to be refrigerated and injected. That would end of my ability to deploy to combat. This set my mind spinning. I begin to think that maybe I'd be able to get a waiver. I'd go on the meds. I'd get stable. Maybe I could come back off of it and continue to serve.

I was plotting this unlikely way forward when the doctor gave me the shocking news. He said, "Son, you're going to need surgery." That was the last thing I expected to hear him say, and it brought me down hard.

He explained that my bowels were obstructed. Apparently, I'd made matters worse by avoiding a medical exam. Crohn's triggers inflammation of the intestinal tract, which causes ulcers to form and become embedded in the intestinal wall. The longer I waited, the worse the ulcers got, causing scar tissue to form and setting up a potentially life-threatening obstruction. This scar tissue could only be removed through surgery. That was it. Leaving his office, I was convinced that my career was over.

FALL OUT

The Crohn's flare-up and my obsession with work also placed an enormous amount of stress on my marriage. At that time, we'd been married a little over three years. We met shortly after my return from Iraq and married quickly after. We then moved to Kansas with her four-year-old son and started a life together.

We had a few things working against us from the start. A few days after arriving at Fort Riley, I was unexpectedly pulled up to be an aide-de-camp, one of the most demanding and stressful assignments that a young officer can have. I would essentially be living someone else's life for the next two years and be traveling non-stop. I'd prepared my wife for military life based on the idea that we'd be part of an infantry unit, meaning she would have the opportunity to build friendships with other spouses in the unit. As an aide, those opportunities were much more limited. I primarily interacted with senior leaders of the organization, who were significantly older than me and my spouse. Although they served as wonderful mentors, the large difference in rank was almost isolating. I knew more colonels and generals than I did captains my own age. This also isolated my wife, and it was difficult to help her build out a real support network.

Despite that, our marriage looked perfect on paper. We rarely argued, we had a nice home, we did lots of things together as a family, and we felt stable. But one thing we always lacked was a true sense of connection and emotional intimacy. This void started to create a lot of distance between us, but we remained committed to trying to overcome it. She fully supported me and my efforts, despite the extreme pace I was maintaining, and she recognized that the work I did had a significant positive impact on the lives of many people.

As the stress increased with the job, however, and as my physical condition deteriorated due to the Crohn's flare-up, I became less present at home. I felt like I was using every ounce of my energy just to make it through the day at work. When I came home, I literally had nothing left. I would go through the motions of being a father and husband, but a lack of intimate connection is difficult to conceal. We slowly grew apart, and it soon felt like we made far better roommates or friends than a married couple.

Although I recognized this and made every attempt I could to work through it, I was so emotionally and physically exhausted from work and Crohn's that my efforts at home went largely unnoticed. They didn't have the impact

I was trying to achieve. There was a larger element, too, that I simply didn't see or allow myself to recognize.

I took our commitment to each other for granted and didn't nurture our relationship. I placed what I was doing at work above my relationship at home. It was a difficult situation. On one hand, I was in the middle of a massive effort that was making positive changes in people's lives. I carried the weight of that responsibility on a national scale, and my wife respected me for it and was fully supportive. On the other hand, it left little room for us.

I was able to sustain the intensity of that pace in the beginning, while still maintaining the marriage, because I was physically healthy. When I was home, I had the energy to maximize our time together. But when Crohn's hit, that energy reserve depleted. I'd come home and would be almost nonfunctional.

This only compounded the extreme sense of disconnect. The day before my appointment with the gastroenterologist, I came home and my wife sat me down to talk. She wanted a divorce. I didn't tell her about the results of the appointment until many weeks later.

In all honesty, I didn't see it coming. I knew that Crohn's was having a major impact on my ability to be present, but I thought our marriage was strong in every other respect.

I was also in the process of preparing for a major career shift within the military, in part, to distance myself from the behavioral health field so I could emotionally reset.

Compassion fatigue was taking a terrible toll on me, and I knew that I couldn't sustain that much longer. I was looking forward to moving to Monterey, California, for sixteen months of intensive Arabic training. I'd been accepted into a program that would prepare me to serve as a foreign area officer in the Middle East, and I planned to put the behavioral health field behind me.

I thought that our marriage would really begin to improve once the stress was reduced and we were out of that environment, but it was too late. She had already rented an apartment and was committed to the divorce.

I didn't say much. I recognized my flaws and respected her reasons. I wanted her to have the opportunity to develop that connection and happiness too, and I knew my career was intense. Beyond that, as bad as it may sound, I was so beaten down—physically and emotionally—that I almost didn't have the energy to care. I helped her and her son move into her new place the next day, and we proceeded with the divorce process. We didn't need to involve any lawyers. The divorce was genuinely amicable and we still maintain a strong friendship to this day.

In the end, I recognized that I was so consumed in my efforts to help other people that I failed to connect with the person closest to me, and I lost my marriage because of it. This is the place where I harbor the most guilt. I could help thousands of people across the globe, but that loses a lot of its meaning when it comes at the expense of those closest to you. It was a hard lesson in life that I was determined to carry forward.

REBUILDING A LIFE

Divorce is hard, regardless of the circumstances surrounding it. When you share that type of a commitment with someone and then watch it fall apart, it feels like a failure. Within the span of twenty-four hours, I learned that I was getting a divorce and probably losing my career due to the upcoming surgery. As I was driving back from the doctor's office, I almost had to laugh at the scope of the situation. I guess when bad things happen, they happen in waves. I was physically and emotionally exhausted.

All questions about my immediate future were put on hold while my gastroenterologist conducted a significant surgery to remove part of my intestinal tract a few months later. The surgery went well, and the surgeon gave me a 50-50 chance of the symptoms returning. Sometimes, having this surgery can result in a lifelong elimination of the symptoms. In other cases, the symptoms relapse. All I heard was the former.

A few days later, I returned to work. The following week, I ran an eight-mile trail race, just to regain emotional leverage over the disease. I was nearing the end of my assignment at Fort Riley and was focused on building a new life in California. At home, it was difficult living in a large empty house alone, but I got through it by staying busy. The divorce wasn't the only thing that shook me over the previous year.

I hit a point of complete burnout and had nothing left. I didn't want to be around people because I didn't have the energy. I needed to reset, and I started to achieve that by remodeling my house. I built a five hundred-square-foot deck, refurbished the hardwood floors, and did major work in just about every room. I had a lot of vacation time built up that I'd never used, and took nearly a full month off between assignments. I spent entire days doing hard and mindless remodeling work. It gave me a healthy outlet and helped me think, reflect, and start to repair the damage I had done to myself over the past several years.

BREAKING THROUGH THE SURFACE

After closing out the final group session and wrapping up my time in company command, I started to prepare for my transition from Fort Riley to the next chapter of my life. As I'd come to learn, the success we had in the unit came at an enormous personal cost. John Musgrave was aware that I was going through a divorce and a major flare-up of Crohn's disease. He'd also seen how hard I'd been pushing it while I was in command. In many ways, John knew me better than anyone, so I really wanted to touch base with him one more time before I left.

I drove over to Lawrence where John lived near Kansas

University. Like all college towns, Lawrence has a little strip of restaurants and bars. We found a friendly Greek place and ordered lunch. We just sat there talking, catching up. I was giving him the layout of what had been going on with me, and, although I was keeping it positive, he sensed something deeper going on.

Out of the blue, he cut me off mid-sentence, looked me directly in the eye, and said, "Josh, you know, there would be a lot of people who would be devastated if you weren't around anymore."

I smiled and said, "Yeah, thanks, John. I know that."

He leaned forward, and said, "No, Josh. Listen to me." His words became very slow and deliberate. "There would be *a lot* of people who would be devastated if you weren't around anymore in their lives."

You can't bullshit John Musgrave. You can't skim the surface or candy coat the details and get it by him. He saw right through my positive spin and understood the gravity of the year I'd just lived through. I think he sensed how close to the danger line I had been. He put his proactive statement out there just in case I needed a steady hand to hold me back and keep me in check.

That's the power of human connection. John had the simple courage to break the surface of a friendly conversation and make a potentially uncomfortable statement. Many people would hesitate to do that. They would think the unpleasant thought, but they wouldn't risk saying it out loud. I understand that. It's hard. But unlike most people, John knew exactly what was at stake.

John and I are members of a small club we call the "I Died and Came Back to Life Club." It's not a club anyone would necessarily want to join, especially in John's case where he was shot in the chest, point blank, deep in a Vietnamese jungle. But once you're in, you see the world differently. You feel a special bond with others in the club. One thing you know for sure is that life is fragile and fleeting—you don't put things off that need to be said right now.

Like me, John was also very active on the speaking circuit—and like me, he had helped many people regain control over their lives and turned them toward recovery. But unlike me, John had been helping others for more than thirty years. When he picked up on the shadow moving in the background of my past year, he was exactly the person capable of calling me on it. At that point in my life, his statement about people needing me was the most important thing that anyone could have said to me. And it wouldn't take me long to find out why.

ROAD TO CALIFORNIA

When it was time to go, I downsized, packed up my truck, and drove cross-country to California. Instead of staying in hotels, I took my time on the trip and camped out at national parks along the route. I hit the Petrified National Forest in Arizona, Zion National Park, and even made a second trip to hit Rocky Mountain National Park. The one-on-one time with nature made me feel like a kid again. I got a beautiful apartment in Monterey overlooking the Pacific Ocean, and started over. I dropped off of the speaking circuit and social media and essentially "went dark." I was looking forward to focusing on nothing but my Arabic studies and starting this new life. But I wasn't in the clear.

The true impact that the previous few years had on me would rise to the surface in unexpected ways. I would occasionally get phone calls from people I'd helped in the past; but, I was experiencing such extreme compassion fatigue that, when I'd see a familiar name appear in the caller ID, I would literally start shaking and pacing around the house. I couldn't answer the phone and had to wait until it went to voicemail. I was terrified that it would be another crisis call—someone reaching out for help—and I knew I didn't have the capacity to help anyone. I didn't have an ounce left to give and I knew it. The thought of even attempting to do so scared the hell out of me. None of these calls turned out to be someone in need. In every case, the caller was just checking in to thank me for everything I'd done for them and to let me know they were doing well. I was glad to learn that they weren't in crisis, but the possibility that they might be was enough to shake me to the core. It would take a few months before I would fully recover from this, but over time I did.

SACRIFICE

Many people ask me if it was worth it. I left Fort Riley with a divorce in one hand and a career-ending surgery in the other. I sacrificed my marriage and my health, and within a year of leaving command, my military career came to an abrupt end due to another flare-up of Crohn's disease. My body and mind were clearly forcing me to slow down after driving myself into a state of exhaustion.

As the distance grew from the military, I found myself increasingly exposed to new perspectives in a new world. Most of this was extremely positive and I appreciated it immensely. In other ways, the "foreign" culture I was now in caused me to forget some important aspects about myself.

When I first wrote this book, I was very self-critical, particularly due to the extreme pace I maintained at Fort Riley. I felt responsible for the loss of my marriage, and in retrospect, it seemed obvious that I was using that pace, that addiction to work, as a way to avoid processing the deepest elements of my own traumatic experiences. I allowed other people to fill my mind with negative beliefs, and heard these things so much that I started to believe them.

But close to the time of my book's publication, in late 2017, documentary producers Ken Burns and Lynn Novick released a major historical documentary titled *The Vietnam War*. John Musgrave was one of the central figures featured throughout the entire documentary series. Almost five years earlier, Ken had caught word of what John and I were doing with the support group at Fort Riley and wanted to capture it on film. The segment his film crew captured for the documentary was the final group session John and I ever ran at Fort Riley before I departed to California.

When you watch this twenty-minute segment, you'll notice that I look terrible. I was thirty pounds lighter, pale, and just coming off the divorce and surgery. I stopped at nothing to help give hope to those who were struggling, and this is what I looked like at the end of that long, exhausting process. I left that unit all but completely broken, with every ounce of energy expended. I went through a lot of emotional turmoil afterward because of it.

Many people told me to stop. To slow down. To take care of myself. But those who know me and those who were part of this unit know that slowing down simply wasn't an option. If I didn't lead this effort, who would? If I didn't make what needed to happen a reality, who would?

When I saw the documentary after it went live, nearly five years after it was filmed, it riveted me. It brought me right back to that place and time—not just mentally, but emotionally. I could literally feel everything about it, and I could feel it within the context of everything that was happening at that time. Seeing the video reminded me of exactly why it *was* worth it. It also reminded me that there was much more to keeping that pace than suppressing my own problems. Frankly, that couldn't have been further from the truth.

Was I fully healthy back then? No. But I was a little further along than some. I was healthy enough to reach back into the trenches and help pull others out along with me, rather than sprinting away from them to work solely on myself, instead. If I didn't do what I did, some of them might not be with us today; as their leader, I had to do everything possible to set the conditions for their success. It's what had to be done at the time. With the military, law enforcement, and first responder populations, we *must* be willing to meet sacrifice with sacrifice.

Today, I still maintain a fast pace and my sense of urgency is greater than ever, but I've also learned how to manage that pace more effectively by continuing to process my own experiences, integrating disciplined wellness practices into my life and relying on the incredible connection I've built with those surrounding me. I didn't have those backstops fully in place back then, but, at the time, I had to do what needed to be done. I don't regret those sacrifices for even a moment.

A DIFFERENT DRUG

All that being said, the situation back then wasn't ideal or sustainable, but not for the reasons you might be thinking. Post-military life helped me unveil even more of the core issues, perhaps through the process of elimination and direct experience more than anything else.

I was maintaining an ultra-fast pace in the private sector

that was comparable to the military. Those who work in environments like Silicon Valley know what I mean. By this point, I was keenly aware of the dangers associated with maintaining this level of intensity. I'd learned a hard lesson coming out of my last assignment and wasn't going to allow my pace at work to mask or conceal my continuing recovery process. In full truth, my awareness of this potential pitfall *did* allow me to avoid it. The intensity was still there, but it was coming from a different place within me. After a few months, I was excelling in my career and felt great. I thought I'd overcome the past, checked that block, and could move forward—but the critical life lesson I still needed to learn was about to surface in ways I never expected. Healing is a journey, never a fixed point in time.

Emotions like shame and guilt are incredibly complex and cannot be underestimated. If nothing else, it's imperative to maintain a certain level of humility toward the unexpected influence they can have over our lives. In my case, they showed their face years before, and after a lot of deeply introspective self-work, I thought I'd defeated them. I was wrong. I didn't realize that they just retreated back into the darkest parts of my soul, hiding in the shadows until they found another avenue to express themselves. This time, it would be through alcohol and unhealthy relationships.

The shield of the story I found myself hiding behind at Fort Riley wasn't necessarily due to the pace I was keeping.

It was, instead, stemming from a deeper internal *need* to assist other people. It developed into an insatiable desire to play that role in the lives of so many others. Back then, I thought this was simply the cost of sacrifice and selflessness, but remained unaware that the very deepest parts of the trauma were in fact driving this. To reach a point of true transformation, I needed to go deeper. The universe was about to slap me around until I got the hint.

Shame is essentially the feeling that we are worth less than others, and I've repeatedly discussed situations throughout this journey where I didn't feel that I deserved to be alive. What better way to compensate for that dark feeling than playing an essential, life-changing role in the lives of others? The shield of my story allowed me to artificially compensate for this internal vulnerability. It's not to say I was doing this intentionally or that what I was doing was wrong—the critical differentiation that needs to be made here is the place it was ultimately coming from. Was I truly only doing this for others, or did I unknowingly *need* to do it for myself? The former is sustainable, the ladder is self-destructive.

For my first few years in the private sector, the speaking circuit wasn't in play anymore and the intensity of helping other people through crisis on a near-daily basis was gone. To compensate for that, I subtly began to gravitate toward destructive relationships. I became a "rescuer," far more concerned about the women I was with than myself. It was a perfect way to fill the void that was subconsciously driving me. When I was in between relationships, alcohol became the substitute. At one point, I was averaging close to ten Jack and Cokes per night.

Unfortunately, neither of these things worked for very long. The relationships always ended disastrously—usually sabotaged by some form of abandonment—and the alcohol use left me feeling, well...hungover. I was able to stop using alcohol on my own accord because I didn't want it to impact my performance at work. But each time a relationship ended, my reaction would grow progressively more severe and more dangerous. I'd fought through several suicidal spirals during this time, and for all of them, the catalyst—not the root cause, but the *catalyst*—was a failed relationship.

For those of us harboring unresolved shame, our Achilles' heel is rejection and abandonment. The late John Bradshaw, in his book *Healing the Shame That Binds You*, says, "There is no greater potential for painful shame than rejection. This is a truism for all relationships. But for shame-based people, rejection is akin to death. We have rejected ourselves; when someone on the outside rejects us, it proves what we fear most: that we are flawed and defective as persons. Rejection means that we are indeed unwanted and unlovable."[3]

---

3   John Bradshaw, *Healing the Shame that Binds You* (Health Communications INC: Deerfield Beach, FL, 247.

The last spiral I was in was extremely bad, stemming from an abrupt and devastating relationship failure. I thought I'd hit rock bottom before, but it was nothing even remotely close to this. I dropped everything and took a one-way flight home to Pennsylvania. I was in such a fragile state that I didn't know what else to do. For three weeks, I paced around the floor of my parents' home for hours at a time. I couldn't stop shaking. I had to force myself to eat. I couldn't sleep; and when I did drift off, I had nightmares and night sweats. I felt as though this experience completely invalidated who I was. I didn't think I'd ever be able to give another talk again. I didn't think I'd ever be able to write this book. I didn't know whether I'd be able to perform my job. I couldn't see past an hour, let alone a full day. It was a complete fog, a situation where I'd reached my absolute limit and felt I'd lost everything. It was almost like hitting the reset button on life and waking up to a blank slate of a world. But it was *precisely* what I needed to uncover the truth behind trauma.

Two things emerged from this experience that set the conditions for true transformation. The first clarified and solidified the true meaning of "human connection" and was realized immediately in the moment of clarity—the epiphany. I looked at my mom, my dad, and my sister, who literally didn't leave my side. I thought about the *hundreds* of people who reached out to me on social media. I thought about the conversations I'd had with my manager and the unwavering support she afforded me. I thought about the dozens of clinicians who offered to help me work through the crisis point. I realized that I was surrounded by the power of human connection everywhere I looked—and it's *always* been that way. Connection wasn't limited to a single relationship, romantic or otherwise. It was and is everywhere.

The second thing that emerged was progressively revealed over the next several months. I walked away from this experience asking the one question I should've been asking myself all along—*why?* Why were my reactions to relationship failures so incredibly severe? Why did they continue to get worse? There had to be something deeper going on that I was missing, and I had to face it in order to stop the cycle. Going back to Bradshaw's words, these situations were clearly indicative that I was still carrying unresolved shame and guilt. As much as I tried to force its resolution in the years prior, I finally *internalized* that my attempts to do so were pushing me further away from it. I had only one choice remaining—to look inward and surrender to it.

RELINQUISHMENT

On the night before Memorial Day in 2017, I was nervous. I was to be the keynote speaker at the San Francisco National Cemetery at the Presidio Trust the following morning. Thousands of people were expected to be in attendance, including Gold Star Families and many dignitaries, and I knew I needed to deliver.

I had given Memorial Day talks before, but there was something special about the energy leading up to this one. The Presidio is an iconic landmark on the West Coast. It overlooks the Golden Gate Bridge in the San Francisco Bay and encompasses the headstones of thirty thousand Americans who are laid to rest there. I knew this talk had to be absolutely perfect to properly honor the sacrifice of our fallen. There was no room for error and I exhaustively rehearsed for a full month prior to its delivery.

My good friend Robert Vera flew in the night prior to attend the event. Robert is the best-selling author of *A Warrior's Faith* and has an incredible perspective on trauma. He's become a mentor for many of our nation's warriors and has made an instrumental impact on my life. I knew having him there in support would give me an added level of confidence.

We got into San Francisco late that night, checked into the hotel, and had a light dinner. But I couldn't contain the anxiety I had about the following morning. I knew the talk cold, but wanted to do a live rehearsal at the Presidio. As a professional speaker himself, he knew exactly what I was feeling. Robert didn't care that it was already approaching midnight. He just said, "Let's go." We got back in the car and drove to the Presidio.

No one else was there. Just the solid white marble

podium and the thirty thousand headstones with American flags draped over them. Standing behind the podium, I could see the Golden Gate pushing through the dense fog that surrounded it. The lights from the bridge illuminated the fog, giving it an eerie orange glow. The wind howled, and with the exception of the lights from the bridge, it was completely dark. Robert and I took a moment to take in and appreciate the hallowed setting that surrounded us. Then he moved out in front of the podium and stood in front of me, mimicking where the audience would be, and I began.

I had to project my voice so Robert could hear because the wind was so strong. It was an unnerving, almost spiritual feeling, and we could both sense the power of the moment. My delivery was perfect. The inflection, the pace, the emotion, everything. Robert just stood there and was looking around, taking it all in, when I said, "Robert, that felt pretty good but I think I need to do it another time, just to be sure."

Robert looked down toward the ground, and then slowly glanced up at the headstones standing before him. A few seconds went by. The wind continued to howl.

He then slowly turned his head toward me, and said, "Josh, you just gave the talk to the people who needed to hear it the most—thirty thousand of them."

We both just stood there for a moment, taking it in and listening to the wind crossing the tops of the redwoods surrounding the cemetery. The headstones were resting peacefully below. His comment riveted me. I didn't need to go through another rehearsal. I got all of the power I needed from the sacred energy that was pouring into us that night.

The next morning as I was speaking, I found myself looking through the crowd and only seeing the headstones and the scene from the night before—the people who needed to hear it the most. As I was closing the talk, I said, "The most powerful way to honor their sacrifice is by allowing their *spirit* to live through us each and every day." At the exact moment I said the word "spirit," the winds suddenly picked up and nearly blew over the flags that were posted on stage. Their presence was there, telling us that it's okay to live. To live *for* them.

That day, I found myself surrendering again, this time consciously and willingly, to the presence of something much greater than ourselves. Part of everything, and nothing. Returning, even briefly, to a sense of inner peace.

Chapter 12

The Darker Soul

SO WHAT EXACTLY IS THE BEAUTY OF THE DARKER SOUL? For that, I turn to Holocaust survivor and world-renowned psychiatrist Viktor E. Frankl. In his famous book *Man's Search for Meaning*, Frankl writes, "Without suffering and death human life cannot be complete. The way in which man accepts his fate and all the suffering it entails, the way in which he takes up his cross, gives him ample opportunity—even under the most difficult circumstances—to add deeper meaning to his life."[4]

All of our experiences shape who we are as people. They allow us to acquire depth, perspective, and wisdom. They broaden our emotional bandwidth and give us the capacity to empathize with others on a much deeper level. This gives us the opportunity to help people, which is where I find the greatest meaning in life and where I find beauty within the darkness.

---

4   Viktor Frankl, *Man's Search for Meaning* (Beacon Press: Boston, 2006), 67

My life has melted me down, reshaped me, and hardened me over and over again. Many of my experiences were extreme and put my resolve to the test. I've been able to overcome a lot, but I can also tell you—unquestionably—that there were many times when I had no resolve left. No desire to continue. No resilience. No sense of self-worth. I've felt completely defeated and broken. I've called into question the purpose of my second life many times because of it.

But as I look back on the past decade and walk through every painful experience, some very clear patterns have emerged that have been the force that kept me going. During the most difficult moments of my life, there were *always* people who had the strength and courage to help me through. They gave me the gift of connection, a gift that I'm happy to pay forward at every opportunity.

Interestingly, many of the people who resonated most closely with me didn't always come from a military background. They were investment bankers and entrepreneurs, teachers and social workers, they were doctors, attorneys, and engineers. They came from every ethnicity, every sexual orientation, and every gender. But they were all people who, at some point in their lives and in their own ways, were exposed to the darker side of human nature. They were people who had the strength to be vulnerable, and that vulnerability is what binds us together at the very core of the human experience.

Trauma doesn't discriminate. It comes in many shapes and forms and it impacts all of us, from every walk of life. Though the nature of our experiences may be very different, the emotions that manifest from them are often very similar, especially when we look at them through the lens of shame, powerlessness, betrayal, and guilt.

If you know guilt, then you've already walked some of the same battlefields as I. If you know shame, then you already know the deepest part of who I am. We need each other to heal. We need a community. As we walk through this final chapter, I'd like to encourage you to always remember the capacity we have to make a positive difference in the lives of others.

A HEALING PATH

Throughout this journey, there were many things I could've done differently. The mistakes I made were plentiful, and the flaws I carry are deep, but the path that I took was ultimately the right path for me. I know that because I'm here. I've internalized both the power of inner strength and the freedom that comes with surrender. We each have to find our own path in our own way, and we each must be ready and willing to heal.

After nearly ten years of navigating through trauma (and many false starts), some central truths have consistently emerged in my ability to overcome. I'd like to share these things with you as we prepare to close this book. A simple awareness of these concepts, in addition to placing some thought into how they might apply to your life, may be enough to help you initiate or continue the healing process.

Maintain Disciplined Wellness Practices. Traumatic experiences can cause us to feel like we're not in control of our lives, but there are certain things we have direct control over, regardless of the emotional state we're in. Three of these items that are of utmost importance are diet, exercise, and breathing. Eating a hormonally balanced diet, conducting anaerobic exercise, and learning how to bring awareness to your breathing patterns all have a direct impact on our physical and emotional well-being. When done consistently and integrated into a daily practice, the combined effects of these three factors drive results far more powerful than any drug.

Every morning, I follow a disciplined practice regardless of how I'm feeling. This includes a high-intensity workout, warming up and cooling down with yoga, and closing with a meditation and breath work sequence. Start small and do it consistently. It will allow you to "win the day" and progressively set the conditions to regain control over your life. If you're looking for a book that walks you through every step of integrating a mind-body-spirit practice into your life, I strongly recommend reading *Firebreather Fitness* by Greg Amundson. I adapted my daily practice directly from his work.

Trauma Isn't Always What It Seems. My healing process

was delayed for years because it was overshadowed by the isolated experience of getting shot and dying. It seemed like such an overtly traumatic experience that many people saw it as the focal point of my recovery. Internally, though, I never felt this experience had a major negative impact on my life. During the incident, there was little to no sense of shame, guilt, or betrayal. Moreover, I was mentally aware that something like this could happen and was well trained to handle it when it did—but I started to believe it *should* be traumatic because of the enormous amount of focus placed upon it by everyone around me. Dying became my convenient scapegoat. All the while, I could sense that something much deeper was burdening me, though I couldn't place my finger on what it was for years.

As I started to bring some light to that dark void, I realized experiences both before and after that incident, even though they didn't appear as traumatic on the surface, were far more challenging for me to navigate than dying itself. The death of my father, abandonment in relationships, the totality of the deployment to Baghdad, the guilt in my ability to heal when others couldn't, and the powerlessness over Crohn's disease were just some of these challenges. The point here is that you must give yourself permission to explore, recognize, and validate the true source of your pain. There's no need for bravado. Sometimes the smallest, most microscopic detail of an experience is enough to make us implode, and uncovering those details is often the catalyst that initiates a true healing process.

Trauma Is Complex. It's nearly impossible to process traumatic experiences if we speak about them only in broad context. "I was wounded," "I was assaulted," "I was abused," are all statements that most would assume to be highly traumatic. In order to heal, however, we have to be willing to dive deeper. We often need to explore the specific details of those experiences to uncover why it's traumatic for each individual person. This is most effectively and safely accomplished in presence of a trained trauma therapist.

When our traumatic experiences remain unresolved, it's normal to view these incidents out of context, blaming and shaming ourselves for decisions we made in the span of microseconds. Cognitive "errors" and even irrational thoughts can develop that compound the level of pain and overtake our lives. There are reasons why we act the way we do. There are reasons why we feel pain. Reconstructing those details can be a long and painful journey, but the new perspective gained from doing so can result in newfound strength that drives contentment for the rest of your life.

Trauma Is Cumulative. The way we respond to situations and people in our lives is largely shaped and influenced by everything that's come before. One event builds upon another—from how we were raised by our parents, to our experiences in school, to our relationships and careers— they're all interrelated. Along the way, traumatic events create cracks in our foundation. If we continue to move forward without repairing those cracks, we end up trying to build the rest of our lives on a shaky foundation. This is why we sometimes have severe reactions to events that are seemingly insignificant.

Finding and repairing the cracks in your foundation requires serious detective work to objectively sort through the facts of your life and explore each incident. Your understanding of the cumulative effect of trauma is critical because many people with unresolved trauma (myself included) begin faulting themselves for their uncharacteristic behaviors and extreme reactions to seemingly minor situations. The reality of what's behind all that is much more complex than anything we see on the surface.

Healing Takes Time. It took nearly ten years for me to be able to say with confidence that "I have only just begun the true healing process." Ten years. It took this long despite being a national advocate for behavioral healthcare, delivering hundreds of talks, helping thousands of others, and regularly interacting with clinical providers throughout. I'm not saying this to discourage you. I'm saying this because it's imperative that we maintain a healthy respect for our experiences and the power they can have over our lives—something which many of us are blinded to while we are suffering. The healing process is a progressive, ever-changing effort that ebbs and flows with life itself—never a fixed point in time. Allow yourself to appreciate the journey.

Be Receptive to Feedback. Sometimes, in the early stages of healing we have to place blind trust in those closest to us. I've mentioned that there were many times when people approached me with concern over my well-being. Often, I wasn't able to internalize what they were saying, but I was still *receptive* to it. I didn't throw out the idea. I maintained a sense of humility and recognized that other people might see warning signs in me that I could be missing. They might know parts of me better than I know them myself. In doing this, I allowed them to plant the healing seeds that would start to grow when the time was right. I certainly could've done many things differently over the past decade, but my receptivity to feedback is what kept me alive. I hope that anyone reading this book can find the strength to do the same.

Build a Network. I didn't hesitate to reach out to people when I found myself pushing emotional limits that were beyond my control. Like me, you might initially hesitate to do so because you don't want to burden anyone else with your problems. This logic is flawed. People who love you—and there are many different forms of love—are typically honored and humbled that you would *trust* them with your experience. In many respects, doing so drops all walls and barriers as you expose your true soul to them. This is a sacred space that the right people in your life will naturally honor and respect. It's important to identify who those people are so you can lean on them when the time comes.

To overcome my resistance to burdening anyone in particular, I wouldn't just call one person in times of crisis. I would call about ten. Sometimes back to back, all day long. At my worst points, even an hour on the phone with someone wouldn't be enough. I'd feel connected and safe on the phone, but the moment I hung up, the pain would creep back in and I'd feel overwhelmed. So I'd call someone else. I'd tell them the same story. I'd get their perspective and feedback. I'd do this over and over again until I was stable. After a day or two of doing this, I was at least out of the danger zone and felt like I had a path forward.

More importantly, I'd find myself amazed—literally amazed—at people's ability to connect with me on such a deep level. Many of them had similar experiences I never knew about, even though they were close friends or family members. This is often just the "stuff" that's never talked about, and something I'm encouraging everyone to find the strength to change. Even when you're utterly convinced that you're alone and that nobody could possibly understand the depths of your pain, there will be someone in your life who'll prove you wrong. But you have to give them the opportunity. Trust in the power of connection.

Suffer Productively. The best definition of therapy that I've encountered to date comes from a clinical social worker named Lori Galperin. Lori and her counterpart, Dr. Mark Schwartz, are the directors of an incredible therapeutic program in Monterey, California, called Harmony Place. I was shadowing a group session that Lori was conducting, when she said, "The purpose of therapy is to help someone suffer productively, as opposed to allowing them to suffer in vain." I can't think of a better, more grounded and realistic way to define this. We're going to experience suffering in our lives. As we overcome those experiences, we can find meaning within that suffering and begin to heal.

It took me years to find myself in the office of Vic Bruner. She didn't "heal" me that day—no one can do that but ourselves—but she did give me the initial insight and perspective I needed to start processing my experiences in a more productive manner, instead of spiraling out of control. Sometimes, perspective is everything. When you're attempting to manage the complex emotional challenges associated with trauma, you may want to consider exploring a few sessions with a strong therapist. It could help you regain control over your life faster and lessen the unnecessary suffering you're experiencing.

Most of what I've mentioned in this section is conceptual. It's my attempt at planting some subtle seeds in your mind that may one day be beneficial to you or someone you care about.

But as I bring this book to a close, I want to emphasize one final and crucial point that highlights the important role all of us can play in helping one another heal.

Trauma Doesn't Discriminate. This world exposes every one of us to suffering of varying degrees, but we can find a positive counterbalance to that pain within each other, through connection, and through love. Although extensive clinical resources exist within the behavioral health field, there is nothing more important than the level of trust we develop with our friends, coworkers, and loved ones. Trust can serve as a gateway into the treatment process. Those seeking treatment are doing so at the most vulnerable and fragile moments in their lives. This requires an enormous amount of personal courage and strength, particularly in the face of a misunderstood and overly stigmatized field. Sometimes, we need reassurance and permission from those we love and trust to find the strength needed to take the next steps. The absence of love and empathy can create destructive feelings of loneliness, isolation, and self-doubt. Reaching this state isn't only a barrier to treatment, it's a barrier to achieving inner peace.

Regardless of one's circumstances, it's never too late to find inner peace—but we have to rely on each other to get there. Giving someone the security of feeling they aren't alone anymore is perhaps the greatest and most selfless gift we can give to another human being in our lifetime. Each of us has the power to do this. So, if you're called upon, don't be intimidated. Leverage your resources, leverage the perspective gained from your personal struggles, and leverage the darker part of your soul to build that relationship. Take the first step down the healing path with them.

To those considering treatment, my message to you

is simple: you are surrounded by support, often in places where you least expect it. You are also surrounded by people who understand your pain, even if you don't believe that right now. Shame is the strongest of demons; it creates a blinding perpetual cycle of self-hatred and doubt. Shame also has a vulnerability, one that can be exploited through the power of human connection. Sometimes in our weakest moments, our only option is to place blind trust in the people closest to us and surrender ourselves to each other and the process of healing. This creates the spark needed to drive the power to heal.

I opened this book with this dedication: "To the people who are suffering from traumatic experiences, and to those who have the courage to help them heal."

The truth is, that's not just a dedication, that's a call to action—from one darker soul to millions of others. If you're suffering from a traumatic experience, it's an invitation to begin or renew the healing process. If someone you care about is suffering, it's an invitation to acknowledge how important your role is in that process. Together, we will change the paradigm.

On behalf of the Darker Souls community, we fully support you and look forward to joining you in this journey. Please join our growing numbers at www.darkersouls.com, and follow us on Facebook @ Darker Souls LLC.

Acknowledgments

I'D LIKE TO THANK MY MOTHER, MICHELE, FOR BEING the strongest woman I know. My stepfather, Degg, for stepping into the lives of two young children and shaping them as you did. To my sister, Melissa, for the journey we took as kids. And to my sister, Kendra, for being the most powerful source of strength for me throughout the years, even though you probably never knew it. You give me hope!

To my high school Junior ROTC instructor, Doug Van Der Pool, for the wisdom and support you provided along the journey and for your dedication to shaping the lives of so many others.

To the West Point Class of 2005. I remain in awe of what our classmates continue to accomplish to "keep freedom alive." I'm humbled to be associated with such an incredible group of people. You've shaped me in more ways than you'll ever know and inspire me to do more. Also a specific thanks to West Point instructors Colonel Mark Conroe,

Dr. Raja Chouairi, and Colonel Rocky Burrell, all of whom had a dramatic impact on my professional and personal development as a young cadet.

To the men and women of 1st Battalion, 8th Cavalry Regiment. There are too many of you to thank individually, but you know who you are. Our camaraderie is etched in stone for eternity. You're the finest officers and soldiers I've ever known.

To Marlon Harper and his family. You will always be remembered and your spirit lives through us each and every day. I hope this work does some justice in capturing the incredible person you were. "Thank you for your sacrifice" doesn't cut it for me—know that I will continue to honor you by the actions I take every day.

To Fort Riley. Specifically, Major General David Petersen, Colonel Kevin Brown, Major Jeff Hall, and Traci Scott for your mentorship, support, and dedication to the members of the team. You had an incredible influence on me then, and you continue to do incredible work to this day. Your spirit kept me alive. Also to the cadre, clinicians, and leaders of the Warrior Transition Unit for your relentless support. Last, to the soldiers who displayed the strength to take on a daunting healing process. You had to place a lot of blind trust in our leadership and I deeply respect the courage you displayed along this journey.

To Victoria Bruner, Dr. Briana Goff, John Musgrave, Steve Goodwin, Phil Randazzo, Dale Fitzke, Dr. Bob Koffman, and the many others who not only supported my journey, but supported countless others as well. Your dedication defines the power of human connection.

To Lisa Ling, for having the courage to shed light on people's darkest moments and bring awareness to situations where few dare to venture. You continue to give people hope by bringing their truth to the surface.

Also, to Ken Burns and Lynn Novick, for recognizing the power of what we were doing at Fort Riley, and for capturing one of the most important moments of my life in such a profound way.

To the many, many people who walked with me through life's most challenging moments. You gave me perspective. You gave me strength. And you gave me the hope to keep moving forward. There are too many of you to name, but my gratitude cannot be more significant. I hope the underlying message of this work demonstrates just how important you are.

To the nonprofit community. Thank you for your continued dedication to filling critical gaps within our system. Special thanks to the teams running intensive and integrative retreat programs at the National Veterans Wellness and Healing Center, led by Chuck Howe; the team at Boulder Crest, led by Ken Falke; and the Permission to Start Dreaming Foundation, led by Leslie Mayne. Thank you for your continued leadership and dedication.

To the first responder professions and emergency medical teams. You understand sacrifice. You live it. You dedicate your lives to serving other people and have the courage to operate "in the arena," often facing impossible situations. My respect for you could not be more sincere. Thank you for all that you do.

To the Patriot Authors Network. To Robert Vera, Jay Dobyns, Jason Redman, Greg Amundson, and Kevin Briggs. All of you have turned extreme experiences into positive messages of hope for others. Your leadership continues to inspire me every day.

Finally, to the team at Book in a Box for helping me get this work out. Any great project takes a team of people surrounding it, and your professionalism and guidance was invaluable. Specific thanks to my editor, John Averill, for the many late-night words of encouragement that kept me going during one of the most emotionally challenging times of my life. Writing can feel like an exercise of insanity. I wanted to throw this entire work in the trash more than once, but I'm glad I didn't. Thanks to you, my publisher, Dan Bernitt, and friend, Charlie Hoehn, for your deeply personal investment in this work from start to finish.

About the Author

JOSH MANTZ is a professional speaker, author, and the CEO of Darker Souls. A 2005 graduate of West Point, Mantz led a successful counterinsurgency operation in Baghdad until a catastrophic sniper attack upended his Army career path in 2007.

In the years since, Mantz has leveraged his combined expertise and unique perspective to help people recover from emotionally traumatic experiences, and is now leading a paradigm shift in the way we think about the moral, ethical, and spiritual implications of life's most challenging experiences. Mantz has been profiled in *The New York Times* and on CNN and FOX News, and speaks professionally worldwide. A native of Pennsylvania, Mantz now resides in the San Francisco Bay area.

Made in the USA
Columbia, SC
19 February 2018